DIANA: FRACTURED FAIRYTALES

By the same author:

Diana

Fractured Fairytales

J. JOHN

KINGSWAY PUBLICATIONS
EASTBOURNE

Co-published in South Africa by SCB Publishers
Cornelis Struik House, 80 McKenzie Street
Cape Town 8001, South Africa
Reg no 04/02203/06

ISBN 0 85476 776 2

Designed and produced by Bookprint Creative Services
P.O. Box 827, BN21 3YJ, England for
KINGSWAY PUBLICATIONS
Lottbridge Drove, Eastbourne, E Sussex BN23 6NT.
Printed in Great Britain.

Diana
Princess of Wales
1961–1997

Contents

Preface

It is intriguing how most of us see what we want to see, hear what we want to hear, say what we want to say. We are selective. We filter our intricate mesh of emotional experiences, prejudices and decisions.

The subject of this book may itself serve as an illustration of the filtering process. Much has been written on Princess Diana in the past decade, much more will be written in the next. I am a Christian, a husband and a father. I therefore write with these filtering factors and emotions. I offer these bread-crumbs as food for thought on Diana, life and death.

I would like to thank Richard Herkes, Publishing Director of Kingsway Publications, who phoned me on the Monday following Diana's funeral, invit-ing me to write this book (we spoke on the phone

every day that week – discussing and deliberating!).
I would also like to thank my dear friend Chris
Russell for his invaluable assistance, his astute
and incisive contribution, amendments and
research. In addition my thanks go to Andy
Economides, a truly great friend, who on numer-
ous occasions inspired me. To Belinda Hollis,
Matthew and Rose Persson for helpful conversa-
tions. Thanks to John and Joan Martin for all the
newspaper cuttings, and to the writer James Mills
for offering helpful suggestions for improvement.

Many thanks to my vicar, Mark Stibbe, and his
wife Alie for their friendship and encouragement.
To all those in our home group, especially to Russell and Corinne Williamson, our leaders. To my
trustees who keep me going. I would like to thank
my colleagues who allowed me time to write when
other work was pressing. To my administrator,
Julia Osborne, who typed and retyped the manu-
script as repeated revisions were made. To my dear
colleague Paul Wilson and his wife Ruth for all
their friendship and support.

It occurs to me to add that wherever I have
borrowed I have tried to give due credit. However, for any material that I may have uncon-
sciously remembered and innocently rewritten, I
ask absolution!

I would like to thank my three sons Michael,
Simeon and Benjamin for the weeks I have been
distracted and preoccupied with the writing of this

book. Special thanks to Michael for letting me write in his attic bedroom – the quietest room in the house!

And my particular thanks go to my wife Killy, who sacrificed hours of companionship so I could write this book. You have been a co-operative assistant during the entire time of writing.

J. John
March 1998

1

The Tragedy of Life Cut Short

For the last two generations the question everyone could answer immediately was, 'Where were you when President John F. Kennedy was assassinated?' or, 'Where were you when you heard John Lennon had been shot?' For our generation there is now a similar question: 'Where were you when you first heard the news of Princess Diana's death?' The death of Diana was one of those occurrences that seems to divide time itself.

The day – Sunday 31st August 1997 – is engraved on our memories. We remember where we were and how we felt. But as for the content of the day – it is a blur. I felt what a lot of people felt: shock, then sadness, and then shock at the depth of my sadness.

The subsequent media coverage of Princess

Diana's death was unprecedented. The constant news bulletins gave us the feeling of being suspended in a tragic drama, which shouldn't, and couldn't be taking place.

The story about the story of Princess Diana's death is one of the biggest media events in history. Even in the first year afterwards the impact on the nation is immeasurable. The story concerns not only the loss of this national figure, but the way in which the nation has reacted, what this reveals about us as a country and a community, what we value and what we long for.

The images will stay with us of that last fateful journey from the Ritz in Paris, and the crushed black Mercedes S-280 Sedan. The car spun out of control after entering a tunnel alongside the River Seine and crashed headlong into the tunnel's thirteenth support pillar, killing Diana, her companion Dodi Fayed and their driver Henri Paul, and injuring their bodyguard, Trevor Rees-Jones. What seems almost certain from the doctors at the scene is that Diana was beyond the point of rescue when help reached her. Some still wonder, pointlessly, whether a seat belt would have made a difference for her as it did for Trevor Rees-Jones.

Death is always sad for those who are left behind – even more so when the circumstances are tragic. The media was stretched to the limit in trying to put into words the pain felt by a nation whose reaction surprised even the most hardened of cynics. 'Tragedy', 'Nightmare', 'Horror', 'Disaster', 'Catastrophe', 'Devastation', 'Terrible beyond imagination' – these were just some of the headlines used by editors.

The tragedy of a life cut short was felt by all. Was it because something so terribly ugly had happened to someone so stunningly beautiful? No, it wasn't that. Was it the feeling that at last she seemed to have found happiness and now even that had been taken away? No, it wasn't really that. Was it the unutterable pain of her two beloved boys, who had already been put through so much, being left motherless? Yes, that was part of it. Was it the way her life was ended? Yes, that was also part of it. Many will never be able to acquit the popular media of blame. Diana was pursued to her death by interfering, disrespectful photographers who had already made her life a misery.

On several levels the futility of her death was felt. A woman who had championed the cause of the oppressed – an icon of compassion and goodness – but whose desperate search for love had also made her a romantic heroine had gone. The possibilities, the dreams, the potential that had been were all wiped out and vanished.

Life cut short is always a sharp and painful reminder of the uncertainty and fragility of life. But this shook the world.

In her emergence from 'shy Di' to the triumphant

public figure of her last days, in her accomplishments, even in her failings and frailties, Diana was one of the pre-eminent personalities of the twentieth century. The unique, the complex, the extraordinary and irreplaceable Diana.

But the memory of her life continues. As Elton John predicted in his song, 'The torch we will always carry for our nation's golden child.' 'Candle in the Wind' now serves as a requiem for the public's sixteen-year fascination with a woman who brought glamour to the House of Windsor.

And the fire of her memory is constantly fuelled. After her death and the wave of Di-mania, she quickly moved from being the focus of grief to the object of a multimillion-pound industry. The Princess of Wales has become an unexpected commodity. As people profit from our seemingly insatiable appetite for all things Diana, even trinkets that bear her name have turned into treasures. Welcome to Diana PLC – videos, books, magazines, even T-shirts, tea-towels, 'antique' bronze busts, 'English rose' porcelain sculptures, commemorative plates and medals. Memorials are money-spinning ventures. Several countries have issued Diana stamps. 'It's a revenue-generating experience,' says stamp dealer and expert Dr Leonard Cohen. 'But it is nothing out of the ordinary: the USA issued 600 million Elvis Presley stamps. It made a ton of money. It is a normal way for a government to make a profit.'

Post-Diana, we quickly returned to business as usual. Tour companies using minibuses take visitors through the tunnel, slowing near the thirteenth pillar where the speeding Mercedes crashed. Nobody expects the memory of Diana to fade quickly, but experts wonder just how long the fascination and business can last.

Princess Diana has joined the hall of fame which features those whose lives were tragically cut short and who have now achieved cult status – Marilyn Monroe, Elvis Presley, James Dean, John Lennon.

Why did we feel Diana's death so keenly?

It is odd to be so sad over the death of a person we didn't realise we cared about. Here was someone we 'knew' in a non-personal way. Diana was known, and yet not known, on a scale never reached before. Visually, she was instantly recognisable. She was the most photographed woman in the world. Her face in close-up entered millions of homes via television – her smile, her eyes in their shy upward glance, every hair of her head immaculately coiffured. Her adoring public knew all about her, without asking themselves how they thought they knew.

Countless people who had some slight connection with Diana were paraded in front of us, and endless stories were recounted of the time 'she shook my hand'. Yet despite all this we didn't know her, or what we knew of her wasn't her. We knew via the media. That was the trouble, of course. We had been told more than we should have. Her privacy had become public property.

It was one of the ultimate ironies: we who loved to read about this woman in the press blamed the very media who had helped us fall in love with her. Without the media, Diana might not have been killed. Without the media, Diana would not have been so greatly loved.

But let us be aware and beware. Diana's death transfigured her own image. Our society is obsessed with image, stars and dream life. This was reflected in the epithets people wrote on cards: goddess – angel of mercy – daughter of the gods – queen – our heroine – a beacon of light in a dark world. Diana, Princess of Wales, gradually metamorphosed into what one tribute outside Kensington Palace called 'our New Saint Diana'. She was canonised by the people if not by the church.

This was real Hollywood stuff. The stars, the cameras, the drama. But the trouble was, this was a tragedy in real time. It wasn't make-believe. There was no body-double in the coffin. The Princess was dead.

We all felt part of it. Her death showed that all of us need someone to look up to. And it's not only because she was like a star that we looked up to her. What really caused the connection wasn't this fantasy life she lived out which we all were so

18

fascinated by. Time and time again people testified that they felt such grief because she was 'one of us'.

Obviously, that isn't true. Very few of us are born into aristocratic families. Certainly not into royalty. Nor do we have the money or the privilege of a princess. The majority of us do not have the access or the opportunity. But neither do we have the intrusion or the harassment. So what did we share? In some way we saw in her life our own experiences of rejection, disappointment, sadness, pain and suffering.

Diana was an outsider. She herself once suggested that her status as a royal outcast made her identify with the disenfranchised. 'I was very confused by which area I should go into,' she told the BBC after her divorce, 'then I found myself being more and more involved with people who were rejected by society and I found an affinity there.' In December 1995 she delivered a speech at her favourite charity for the homeless saying, 'It is truly tragic to see the total waste of so many young lives, of so much potential. Everyone needs to be valued. Everyone has the potential to give something back, if only they had the chance. Each time I visit, I am appalled at the dangers young people face on the streets and how vulnerable they are to exploitation.'

Linda Grant, a columnist for the *Independent on Sunday*, wrote, 'What struck me was the way she touched a series of bases in the lives of everyday women. She clocked them up one by one; she came from a broken home, she married so young, she suffered post-natal depression, she had eating disorders, fell in love . . . he betrayed her . . . and which of us hasn't shared at least one of those experiences?' The 500 or so people who followed the coffin symbolised in a very real way the chord she struck – that of being outsiders.

Her work was among outsiders – the casualties of HIV, the homeless, those with cancer, and victims of the carnage caused by land mines. And then she died 'outside' – outside her country, outside marriage and outside the Royal family.

Diana's sincere sympathy for those in need remained constant. She logged thousands of miles each year in support of her causes, even travelling to dangerous locations in Bosnia and Angola to draw attention to the plight of civilians disabled or bereaved by land mines. Diana only did what so many charity and voluntary workers do around the world every day – but she chose to when she could so easily have ignored the unglamorous communities of the world.

In 1987, when many still feared AIDS could be contracted through casual contact, she calmly offered her ungloved hand to a sufferer at a London hospital. 'You can shake their hands and give them a hug,' she later said of people with AIDS. 'Heaven knows, they need it.' This act of kindness advanced the cause of tolerance immeasurably. Royal reporter Judy Wade called it 'the most important thing a royal has done in 200 years'. In 1993 she reached out to touch lepers in Nepal to show, she said, 'that they are not reviled'.

The Princess was patron of the Leprosy Mission, which attempts to minister to the world's twelve million victims of leprosy. Most of the medical advances in leprosy have come from the work of Christian medical missionaries – they solved leprosy's riddles, exposed its myths and developed effective treatments. Yet leprosy rarely attracted much media attention until Princess Diana became involved. In her last interview, Diana told *Le Monde*, 'Nothing gives me more happiness than to try to aid the most vulnerable of this society. Whoever is in distress who calls me, I will come running.'

Diana's weaknesses became her strengths. They allowed millions of ordinary people to identify with her, and made her responsive to the vulnerable and maimed. Diana's experience of personal sadness from early childhood produced not bitterness but insight into the human heart, and a desire to help others. Princess Diana had the ability to speak a universal language of love. She had an unconquerable belief in the power of love to answer and overcome the darkest ills of the world.

Paradoxically, despite her oft-repeated claims of desiring a simple life, she also enjoyed and held on to all the privileges of privilege. Diana revelled in her designer-suited jet-setting lifestyle.

When her friend, clothes designer Gianni Versace, was murdered, it was said that he had fused the worlds of fashion, rock and movies. To this the Princess added royalty.

The good and the great

Remarkably, other prominent people died around the same time – people who had lived full and inspirational lives marked not for their vulnerability but for their achievements.

The night before Princess Diana's funeral the news came through that Mother Teresa of Calcutta had died. Princess Diana's death somewhat eclipsed that of Mother Teresa's – although Mother Teresa would not have been remotely concerned about that. The two most famous women in the world had died within the space of a week. One life ended far too early, the other life came to its peaceful conclusion. In her biography, *Mother Teresa: Beyond the Image*, Anne Sebba writes that Diana 'identified herself very closely with Mother Teresa's philosophy and was known to be a great admirer'. Mother Teresa was reported as saying that Diana was 'like a daughter' to her.

Mother Teresa died at the age of eighty-seven. The youngest of three children, Gouxha ('Rosebud') Agnes Bojaxhiu was born on 27th August 1910 at

Skopje, Albania. At eighteen she left home to enter the Order of Loreto in Ireland. There she adopted the name Sister Mary Teresa after St Thérèse, 'the little flower', who in 1897, at the age of twenty-four, had died of tuberculosis in a convent at Lisieux. She heard God's call to a specific work while on a train travelling from Calcutta to Darjeeling. At that point she was a nun teaching at a school in Calcutta. Years later she recalled, 'I heard the call to give up all and follow him into the slums to serve him among the poorest of the poor. I knew that it was his will, and that I had to follow him.' So the Order of the Missionaries of Charity was founded in 1950.

Cardinal Basil Hume called her 'a unique example of genuine holiness'. He added, 'The utter sincerity with which she lived out her faith gave her an energy and radiance which is unforgettable.' Mother Teresa dedicated herself to her work with a minimum of fuss and little concern for image.

Life seldom linked Mother Teresa, eighty-seven, and Princess Diana, thirty-six, despite a much-reproduced photograph of their last meeting, earlier in the year. But coincidence of timing links them in death. Rarely had the founder of the Missionaries of Charity seemed such a celebrity, or the Princess so saintly. Because they had both highlighted the plight of the poor and vulnerable, comparisons that would otherwise never have occurred suddenly became inevitable.

Mother Teresa was the saint of the gutters, Princess Diana was the saint of the media. Mother Teresa was celebrated for some fifty years of work among the poor. That brought her the Nobel Peace Prize, but not the kind of adulation that attended the death of the Princess. Princess Diana was stunning. Mother Teresa was selfless. Princess Diana suffered despite the riches that surrounded her. Mother Teresa found peace despite the suffering that surrounded her. The older woman died possessing only three saris (woven by lepers from one of her homes in Calcutta), a small crucifix, a wooden wash bucket, one worn sweater, and a much-thumbed Bible; the younger one left an estate worth millions of pounds, and had already auctioned many of her designer dresses at Christie's.

Dichotomies abound – the spiritual and the material life, self-sacrifice and self-indulgence, inner radiance and external glamour. This is not to diminish Princess Diana. It is only to note a difference between a noble life well lived and the life of a noble well cultivated.

One author criticised Mother Teresa for consorting with dictators and other less-than-perfect characters. (A certain carpenter from Nazareth was accused of similar crimes.) But Mother Teresa's legacy leaves us speechless. She proved that faith could indeed move mountains. Today, Mother Teresa's Missionaries of Charity operate 450 centres in 130 countries. They feed half a million families a year, her schools teach 20,000 slum children, her clinics treat 90,000 lepers. More than 27,000 people who might have died on the streets of Calcutta have met a dignified end in her hospices for the dying.

Through the years, Mother Teresa's unceasing devotion and hard work gnarled her hands, lined her face and bent her back – she was only 4ft 10in tall – creating the photographic icon that challenged the conscience of the world.

The Pope described her as an 'unforgettable figure'. He said that Mother Teresa had helped 'life's defeated to feel the tenderness of God'. In the Roman Catholic way of things it is likely that Mother Teresa will be nominated for official sainthood after the requisite five-year waiting period.

Mark Tully, in *The Observer* dated 7th September 1997, wondered why Mother Teresa attracted so much admiration. The answer, he said, showed one of the ironies of this generation: 'We may not have much time for religion ourselves now, but we do seem to be fascinated by saints.' It is a strange society which appeases its sedated conscience by admiring from the safety of its own home the work of an elderly woman caring for the dying.

Certainly, it was true that she knew how to cope with the media. She had a very direct way of dealing with the press, and made it quite clear that her main aim wasn't publicity for her own sake: 'Celebrity has been forced on me. I use it for the love of Jesus. The press make people aware of the poor, and that is worth any sacrifice on my behalf.' Both Mother Teresa and Princess Diana used their fame as a tool to increase the visibility of the poor, the sick and the victimised. By the early 1990s, Buckingham Palace listed the Princess of Wales as a patron of no fewer than ninety charities.

Mother Teresa's death wasn't a tragedy in the way Princess Diana's was. She had been ill for quite some time, and so there was no genuine shock over an untimely passing away. But there certainly was mourning and sadness. There was concern and apprehension about whether her legacy could be sustained. There were even different opinions on her contribution to the twentieth century.

Though both women's deaths caused our hearts to hurt, our response to each was different because they had affected us in different ways. Perhaps it's because Mother Teresa did what we all felt we *should* be doing, while Princess Diana did what we all felt we *wanted* to do. What is certain is that the death of these two women caused us to re-appraise the place of those less fortunate than ourselves. What was best about these two women was what they did for others. If Diana was a 'Candle in the Wind', Mother Teresa was the 'Flame in the Gutter'. Mother Teresa appealed to noble spiritual instincts while Princess Diana evoked secular desires. But in reality, few of us wanted to be either Mother Teresa or Princess Diana. We could fantasise romantically about their lives without doing their arduous or glamorous work, enduring the pain of service or the misery of always being treated as an exhibit.

None of us would dispute the good and courageous work of Mother Teresa, but how many of us envied her chaste life? Mother Teresa protected the bodies of others while risking her own in a profound commitment to Jesus, her Lord. Princess Diana, by contrast, decorated her body with the latest fashion and finest jewels – ultimately worth no more to her than a pebble on the beach at St Tropez where she had sunned her body a few days earlier.

In our secular age, the material life of Princess Diana is more readily understood than the spiritual one of Mother Teresa. As we reflect on Mother Teresa and Princess Diana, we also reflect on ourselves and all that each of us has in common with saints and sinners.

But it wasn't simply the death of Mother Teresa which added to the poignancy of the Princess's death; another death around midnight of the morning of her funeral brought even more consternation to those attending the service. The world lost another of the century's major players. Sir Georg Solti, the most distinguished conductor of the century, died suddenly while on holiday.

Georg Solti was a man who contributed much pleasure to society. His recording career spanned over fifty years, during which he featured on more than 250 records. His time at the Royal Opera House throughout the 1960s is still regarded as a high point in terms of music. He won more Grammy awards than any other musician – popular or classical. The reason for his appeal was obvious: as well as being a brilliant conductor he had a personality which commanded attention and respect. Each performance was new. 'I'm always changing,' he said. 'I never listen to my records – never. I do not want that.' He always wanted to move on, to make headway.

But like Diana, he was an intensely private man, devoted to his family, who would travel hundreds of miles just to be with them. He was also one who lived life to the full, especially in his later years. Instead of reducing his creativity, he continued to think of new projects. 'Only in the last fifteen years have I really begun to study music profoundly,' he admitted. Harvey Sachs, with whom Solti co-wrote his memoirs, said, 'His desire to give himself to his art was phenomenal, and inspiring.'

Psychiatrist and philosopher Dr Viktor Frankl also died in the same week as Princess Diana, Mother Teresa and Sir Georg Solti. Dr Frankl died at the age of ninety-two in Vienna, Austria. His book, *Man's Search for Meaning*, sold more than two million copies in twenty-six languages. The book is based on his experiences in four Nazi concentration camps. When he entered Auschwitz, the Nazi guards stripped him and shaved his whole body in an attempt to deprive him of all human dignity. But despite everything that was done to him, he would not relinquish his humanity, his conscience, or his faith. He returned to civilised life to counsel people to discover meaning by serving God through caring for others, by good deeds and enjoying nature.

Thus in one week in the late summer of 1997, the twentieth century lost four inspirational people, who in their own ways were heroines and heroes to many. They touched lives with the beauty of their faith, their personalities, their actions and their art. Their lives do not call each one of us to hit the headlines, or make a splash, to be remembered with long obituaries in the national papers, or times of public national mourning and grief. But they show us how different lives affect the world in different and similar ways. Life is not valued by how much of it is lived, or what is amassed in the short time we walk the planet, but by what we live for, by the things we stand for, by the extent to which we reach out and touch others with the graces and gifts we have been given.

We each react to death in different ways. Time and time again on the television and radio I heard people saying, 'I have to go down to Diana's funeral. I've got to be part of it. I must be able to say I was there.'

This compulsion showed not only our desire to have someone to share our weakness and sense of alienation. It showed we wanted to be part of something bigger. People want to be part of history, to be able to say they were part of a movement, an event, which will for ever be in the memory of a whole nation, and even many nations.

Think of the all-night queues. Would so many people have joined them if they had only had to wait ten minutes? Wasn't the waiting one of the major factors? To be able to claim, 'I was there. I waited.' To be able to make a positive contribution. The queues outside the palaces caused the poet Carol Ann Duffy to imagine that 'History was a giant, shaken from sleep by love'.

We want to play a part in some momentous occasion. Here, at last, was a chance to prove that we could show sympathy, we could be included in something good and right.

Princess Diana's death took from us someone we wanted to feel part of. This woman belonged to the people. She struck such a chord because her life-style on the one hand was what we all aspired to, but strangely, on the other hand, the true nature of her life reflected the reality of our brokenness.

And so the British nation – and much of the world – found a new figurehead, a heroine to champion the cause of brokenness, and a focus for our sense of alienation from a world that has lost touch with yesterday's certainties.

Her death revealed that even the British now value a show of emotion. And it revealed what kind of religion people feel most 'works': the need for flowers, candles, toys, books – something to do, something to demonstrate. It is a mixture of ancient and modern – of hymns and Elton John, of web sites and silence.

2

Good Grief

What did we think was the proper way to mourn someone we never really knew? First, we talked endlessly, assessing what was truly good. Then we fell silent, gathered around televisions or in the streets and simply watched. Queen Elizabeth took the extraordinary step of making a live, televised speech to assure her subjects that 'we have all been trying in our different ways to cope'.

'She never ever knew she was this popular. If only she'd have known how much she was loved when she had been alive.' This comment was expressed over and over again by the family and close friends of Diana, Princess of Wales when they saw the extent of the nation's grief. It was such a shame, they said, that she had never had any idea of just how popular and highly regarded she was.

'The spring has gone out of the year,' declared an ancient Greek General mourning the loss of young soldiers, and that was very much the mood in the week of Princess Diana's death.

It is the character rather than the scale of grief which has been unique. Millions mourned just as deeply the death of Queen Victoria, King George V (it was recorded that 15,000 fainted during his funeral) and Winston Churchill, but these deaths did not cause people to feel pain. When each one of them died there was a sense that their work had been completed. The death of Diana was premature, sudden, horrifying, and so its effect was traumatic. Acceptance of death brings peace. This death was hard to accept, so hearts were restless.

Grief on this scale could not be ignored by the government. Prime Minister Tony Blair appropriated the Princess as the symbol of a spontaneous New Britain not afraid to cry and show emotion.

As the nation felt weighed down by such a cloud of sorrow we hushed the voices which pointed out that those who were expressing so much sadness were often the ones who had made it *their* business to find out *her* business. But it was true. We who felt anger at those terrible tabloid and paparazzi photographers were the ones who had caused her to be pursued relentlessly, because if there wasn't a huge market for their pictures, they would not be making a living. Someone buys the publications that print those shots of bathing-suit-clad celebrities frolicking. It was we who bought the papers to see the pictures of the make-believe princess. By doing so we in effect demanded she be hounded in the way she was so that we could discover what we didn't need to know about her. There is an easy way to put these photographers out of business: just say *no*. But until that happens, and as long as there is such an enormous demand for their work that the tabloids will pay colossal fees for it, the paparazzi will keep snapping.

Was our grief tinged with guilt? The emotions expressed around the nation, even the world, in the autumn of 1997 were incredibly mixed. The dream had ended, and somehow we wanted to give vent to our feelings of sadness, betrayal, shock and hurt. The problem was that we had not been taught how to. In an article printed in *The Observer* on 7th September 1997 Robert McCrum wrote:

In the past, the fierce and troubling emotions that death stirred up were soothed by ritual formulae of speech and action, whose function was to supply necessary comfort. But not any more. Almost every public utterance this past week suggests that, while we have words and phrases for virtually everything, we have lost touch with the language of grief.

One of the reasons we have lost touch with the language of grief is that we have not dared to let death touch us. Our modern society has made death a taboo. Death has replaced sex as the great unmentionable. The French historian Phillipe Aries wrote this of those who mourn: 'A single person is missing for you and the whole world is empty. But no one has the right to say so aloud.' The model of the ideal mourner is one who doesn't show grief, who keeps a stiff upper lip. We tend not to legitimise the need to be sad.

The media has had a large part to play in distancing us from death. Initially judged responsible for Diana's death, it was now key in providing us with images to intensify our mourning. Before Diana's death we had not been able to rely on the media to depict death in any detail. Although death was reported, it was invariably at arm's length, and you could always change the channel or turn the page. In the week of Diana's death you couldn't. Whereas previously we could depend on the media not to confront us with the physical nature of death and the grief it creates, suddenly it became the stage for it. Usually all this stuff happened off camera in the wings. Now this was all there was. The extraordinary thing in that first week of September was that those who had taken it upon themselves to shield us most from grief and death did an about-turn and gave it mass exposure.

Diana embodied much of what we hope for. So how did a generation sold on life find a place for death? A society which believes that death is the worst thing that can happen to anyone was obviously paralysed by fear when a mirror was held up to its face. All we could see for a time was the horror in our own eyes.

Few of us will forget the images of a nation mourning. No longer was grief a private emotion but rather the opposite – the attitude became 'let it all happen in public'. The British people are usually noted for their reserve, and have prided themselves on their restraint and proper behaviour for generations. This made the spontaneous outpouring of grief in the wake of Princess Diana's tragic death difficult to explain.

The 1,200-word eulogy delivered by Charles, Earl Spencer, at the funeral of his sister Diana received accolades from the public. Standing in the pulpit of Westminster Abbey, he poured out frank personal sentiments that one simply doesn't utter in front of the sovereign. His 'complex' and 'radiant' sister, the 33-year-old Earl said, had led a 'bizarre' life since marrying Charles. He went on to claim that Diana hardly needed the title of Her Royal Highness, the one denied her after the divorce, 'to continue to generate her particular brand of magic'.

A week after the funeral, Buckingham Palace had received 500,000 letters and 580,000 e-mail messages of sympathy. The leader of the Conservative Party, William Hague, suggested that Heathrow Airport be renamed Diana Airport. The Chancellor of the Exchequer, Gordon Brown, was said to be seriously considering a proposal that the August Bank Holiday be called Diana Day. Letters to newspapers revealed that people thought commemorative coins should be issued, and that fountains, bridges and hospitals should become memorials to Diana.

There is a deep human need to come to terms with the tragic dimension of life, and to purify our emotions by exposure to it. It was this need which was in part being met by the remarkable displays of grief.

The strength of public opinion was reflected when three foreign tourists were sentenced to jail for taking teddy bears from the tributes to the Princess which had been heaped up on London pavements. These incidents made lead stories (none in fact served their sentence, but one was punched by an onlooker as he left the court). The price of wholesale flowers rose by 25 per cent in London markets, despite flowers being flown in from Holland, Israel, Africa and South America to meet the unprecedented demand. By

9th September, 10,000 tons of flowers were piled outside the Royal palaces. Estimates of the number of floral tributes reached fifty million. Flowers sent to Althorp Park entirely carpeted the island in the lake after it became Diana's burial place. In all, about 15,000 tons of non-floral tributes were left including cards, trinkets, teddy bears and pieces of crockery bearing Diana's picture. Books of condolence were opened in St James's Palace, then around the country, then around the world. When the forty-two which had been signed at her home, Kensington Palace, were closed on 21st September, they contained 300,000 signatures. By the end of September three million CDs of Elton John's 'Candle in the Wind', which he had first sung at the funeral, had been sold in the UK (twenty-one million worldwide). The press clippings agency Durrants said that coverage in the world's magazines and newspapers had far exceeded that generated by any other event anywhere in the world at any time in history.

'Until this year it seemed as if the old values were for ever to hold sway,' said Martin Jacques in *The Observer* the day after the funeral. But a 'floral revolution' had taken place. He continued:

For a week the biggest and most spontaneous popular movement since the second world war has swept all before it – as its agenda, like all popular revolutions, changed the day. Once we were a stuffy and inexpressive nation, now we have come of age. We now know, apparently, how to show our emotions and grieve in public. After all, the national bereavement counselling service CRUSE had to open a special help line. Could grief for one woman cause all this?

There was a vast new Internet mainstream casting about for a way to express a profound sadness and finding it literally at its fingertips a 'web of tears'. A week after the accident, the Infoseek web directory listed more than 500 sites devoted to Diana. Most of these sites offered 'guest books' to which thousands more have sent heartfelt e-mails. Just a week after America Online set up a condolence bulletin board with a promise to pass on the mails to the Royal family, more than 135,000 users had responded.

The astonishing response to the death of Princess Diana has defied explanation by any commentators on the nation's psychology. Tragedy brings people together. The death of Princess Diana was certainly a good test of this truth. Nowadays neighbours rarely know each other, so the impromptu reaction allowed people who were strangers to collectively acknowledge a tragedy that hit painfully close to home. The response to Princess Diana's death was created by private citizens who needed a way to deal with a public disaster.

The closest examples we have in recent years are in response to those killed in a national disaster. The 1980s saw a number of such disasters: the fire in 1985 which killed over forty Bradford City football fans, the inferno at King's Cross Underground station in 1987 in which thirty died, and, above all, the Hillsborough football stadium disaster in which ninety-four were crushed to death, and 170 were injured. An abiding painful image from Hillsborough is the great mass of red scarves, hats, shirts and other mementoes adorning railings and filling Anfield football stadium, the home of the stricken and wounded Liverpool club whose supporters had died while attending a match against Nottingham Forest at Hillsborough in Sheffield.

After the tragic and grotesque Hungerford shootings in 1987 when one man shot dead fourteen and wounded fifteen, one of the hundreds of wreaths left on the steps of the town hall read, 'To those who fell.' A more permanent memorial was created when an empty field in Centre Moriches, New York – the town nearest to the coast where TWA Flight 800 exploded in 1996 – was transformed into a garden with a brick path bearing the names of the 230 dead.

Our model of how to grieve and express our feelings perhaps evolved from the spontaneous desire to honour the war dead. The Cenotaph in Whitehall that Princess Diana's coffin passed on its way to Westminster Abbey was erected by popular demand as a lasting memorial to those who died fighting for their country in World War I. Even in 1919, the British demonstrated that they were capable of emotion which officialdom regarded as essentially un-British.

How is grief best defined?

Death, this 'most natural yet unnatural of events', inflicts a sense of loss we call 'grief' or 'bereavement'. The term bereavement comes from the word 'reave', which means to 'ravage, rob and leave desolate'. The grief we feel is caused by our loss, which plunges the heart into mourning. Mourning is the process of adapting to the losses in our life. Through the complex and personal process of mourning, we acknowledge the pain of loss, feel the pain and then live past it. How each of us mourns depends upon our state of readiness and our perception of the loss. The one thing anyone experienced in working with bereaved people will tell you is that every person feels grief differently. Colin Murray Parkes, in his much acclaimed study *Bereavement*, isolates four main phases of grieving: a phase of numbness, shock and partial disregard of the reality of the loss; a phase of yearning, with an urge to recover the lost person; a phase of disorganisation, despair and gradual coming to terms with the reality of the loss; a phase of reorganisation and resolution.

Often there are physical reactions, but even if this is not the case, grief is not a tidy process. Typically, in a major bereavement, the shock lasts up to two weeks, and the whole process of recovery can take some two to four years. Working through grief does not proceed in a straight line either; in fact, one can often feel hijacked by it. One of the most moving pieces of writing on the subject of grief is C. S. Lewis' fine book, *A Grief Observed*. He wrote this book in the first months after the death of his wife Joy from cancer. In it nothing is clearer than grief's grip on the recently bereaved lover:

> Tonight all the hells of young grief have opened again; the mad words, the bitter resentment, the fluttering in the stomach, the nightmare unreality, the wallowed-up tears. For in grief nothing 'stays put'. One keeps emerging from one phase, but it always recurs. Round and round. Everything repeats. Am I going in circles, or dare I hope I am on a spiral? But if a spiral, am I going up or down it?
> (*A Grief Observed*, p. 46)

Emotions caused by the death of a loved one are very powerful. If these emotions are not faced, experienced, and dealt with, they will end up being a destructive force in a person's life. To fail to face them is to ignore reality.

In 1969, Dr Elisabeth Kubler-Ross, a pioneer researcher on bereavement, published her classic book, *On Death and Dying*, which categorises the coping mechanism of death as a series of five distinct stages: denial and isolation, anger, bargaining, depression, and finally acceptance.

Whether the loss of a loved one is expected or unexpected, the first and most common reaction is shock and denial. This may prompt either vocal or silent weeping. We may feel bewildered, startled, confused, and unable to believe that the loss has occurred. Some may even experience a severe gut-wrenching pain deep inside.

The next phase is a period of intense pain. Feelings of anxiety, panic, helplessness and hopelessness surface. The volume of these feelings makes the mourner either lethargic or hyperactive, and gives them a desire to express anger even though at the same time they are feeling guilt. This is particularly true if we never had an opportunity to put things right, express our love and say our goodbyes. In our despair, when our hearts are heavy, we may continually wonder with deep regret why we didn't call or visit more often. Because the mind is so preoccupied with these thoughts, and the heart stirred with countless emotions, many people become agitated while they sleep and experience disruptive dreams.

Following the initial shock, desolation and anger, the mourner reaches a phase of adjustment, partly because there has to be a change of routine. For the loved one death is an ending, but for the survivor it means a new beginning. As we come to terms with our loss and accommodate the necessary changes we begin to move on.

What does grief feel like? One of the most successful British films of recent years was *Four Weddings and a Funeral*. At the funeral, a poem by W. H. Auden was read, and it has been a favourite ever since. The poem conveys the feeling that the whole world should be aware of the loss, that the focus of everything has gone. One line adapted from the poem was found written on a card left with a bouquet following Diana's death: 'She was my North, my South, my East, my West.'

There can be little doubt that those who knew the Princess personally felt this kind of grief. Outside of that circle of family and friends, what kind of grief were people feeling?

Did we really grieve?

Obviously we must acknowledge that judging the quality of another person's grief is a risky enterprise. But I would beg the question here: Was the nation experiencing real grief, especially bearing in mind everything that we have just considered about the grieving process? Certainly there was numbness and shock at the initial tragic news. There was denial that such a thing could happen and a longing for the Princess to be alive still. But it was not genuine grief – the grief which grips your stomach, the agony which consumes everything. We felt a form of grief with the torment taken out. This isn't to say we were putting it on or that our emotions weren't real. However, there was no generally sustained period of sadness. Did we mourn for ourselves? For the death of a dream? One interesting thing to note is that we all returned pretty quickly to business as usual.

As we saw, death affects people in different ways. Regrettably, the fact that our reactions differ did not seem to be recognised. The papers, from the broadsheets to the tabloids, in the middle of the week following the accident demanded that the palace and royals 'share' their grief. The queues of people waiting to lay flowers or sign the books of condolence were also vociferous in their complaints. They were showing their grief in public, so why not the Royal family? When Prime Minister Tony Blair stepped in to defend the action of the House of Windsor, seemingly marooned in Balmoral, he assured us, 'We must remember the Royal family share our grief.'

But whose grief was it? Could we justifiably call it 'our grief'? And does true grief dictate to those closest to the dead person just how they must be expressing their emotions? As Decca Aitkenhead of *The Guardian* said:

It is very hard to see what right the public and media have to condemn the way in which the Royal family are choosing to grieve. They are among the small number of people actually enduring the real tortured pain of personal bereavement and are entitled to bear their grief in any way they wish.

There was an assumption that because we laid so many flowers and wrote messages on cards we had the right to demand the same public show of grief.

Nineteen hundred mourners packed Westminster Abbey and one million others gathered in London on 6th September for the funeral service. In Britain thirty-one million people watched the funeral service on television – over half the population. More than two billion watched worldwide – the largest audience in the history of television.

Watching, as I did, and crying, as I did, was not an accurate indicator of grief, however. Social commentator Ian Jack offered the following reflection:

This was recreational grief ['look-at-me grief' as the writer Julian Barnes put it]. It was enjoyable and promoted the griever from the audience to an on-stage part in the final act of the opera, which lasted six days. It was grief with the pain removed, grief-lite.

But, yes, we did feel sorrow. The next question, though, is: Who were we feeling sorrow

DIANA

for? Princess Diana's death showed that people
need something to release their pain. As
Suzanne Moore said in the *Independent on Sunday*,
'Like so many people I wept for this loss and
the other losses it brought back to me.' Some
extraordinary reactions were reported. One man
admitted he had cried more at Diana's funeral
than at his father's eight years earlier. Another,
whose wife of forty years had died of cancer in
the spring, confessed that although he had not
shed tears over her death he found himself
doing nothing but crying at the news of Diana's
accident.

If we were so moved, what must have Prince
William and Prince Harry been feeling? In the
film *Ordinary People* the psychiatrist makes an
astute comment when he tells the anguished
Conrad regarding the tragic drowning of his
brother, 'If you can't feel pain, you're not going
to feel anything else either.' Only a few who
were really close to Diana can have experienced
her absence by walking into a room expecting to
find her there and seeing she was not. The loss
to the Princes of their mother is inestimable. She
is unquestionably irreplaceable to them. An
added complication for them is their own position, and the circumstances of their mother's
death.

Diana was a close and involved mother who left
her sons a legacy of love. She raised William and

Harry to be royal and real. The Princes received what they most needed when they were young, and that has given them a certain resilience that will stay with them for the rest of their lives.

Teenagers are usually able to understand what it means to lose a person they loved. However, for the Princes, along with that understanding arises the real fear that if such a tragedy happened to their own mother, a Princess, it could certainly happen to anyone, including themselves. The Princes are dealing with their fragile mortality at a time in their lives when their peers believe they are immortal. My prayer is that Prince William and Prince Harry will always be able to express their feelings and learn to live with the loss of their mother rather than trying to replace her.

When a branch is cut off a fruit tree, the tree will survive, but it is for ever changed. It will no longer have its original shape – it will have an empty space. However, it will blossom in due course, possibly with greater vigour. May the Princes continue to blossom despite the empty space.

Although it is difficult to define the overall response to Princess Diana's death, it seems to have combined newly evolved rituals of mourning in times of national disaster with affection for the British royalty. Being un-British is a very British thing to do, now and again!

3

Fractured Fairytales

At one time or another, every child dreams of being a prince or a princess. It is not surprising really. In childhood we are told stories about princesses who can feel a pea through seventeen mattresses, or frogs that turn into princes when kissed, or kitchen maids who discover they are of royal birth. And this imagination is fuelled by images from Walt Disney's cartoons, and plays in which school children take part.

In the summer that Diana died, for the first time since 1642, William Shakespeare's plays were performed in the Globe Theatre – the theatre for which they were originally written. After three and a half centuries this theatre had been reconstructed on the original site, and to the original plan. Princess Diana's life had all the ingredients of great Shakespearean theatre – love, pain, adultery, scheming and scandal. And her tragic end, so sudden, gave a Shakespearean twist to what began as a beautiful fairytale.

On Saturday afternoons I used to watch a popular television show which made dreams come true. Jimmy Saville, the host of the show, was the genie of the lamp who gave children their one wish. What was the most popular request? To be a princess for a day. But to be a princess for the rest of your life? Well, it's a wonder if post-Diana anyone will want that.

On the day she died, Prime Minister Tony Blair gave Diana the title now frequently used in connection with her – the People's Princess. This was what she always wanted – to be Princess not by birth or marriage but by popular consent.

As the People's Princess, Diana lived in the fantasy world people of this generation want to escape to, but at the same time she was faced with the uncomfortable realities of life that people long to escape from.

Fact and fiction

The people who are most important to us are instrumental in making us who we are. Our most powerful emotions – love, anger, care, gratitude, rivalry and hero-worship – arise from our interaction with other people. A major part of our inner life is taken up with people, as they loom large in our memories, fantasies and hopes.

Our intense reaction to the death of Diana made us aware that the people who most shape us are not necessarily those we live close to, not necessarily the members of our family or those we meet. A strange feature of our culture is that daily we identify with a large number of fictional characters. So the characters in a long-running soap about the life of ordinary Londoners or Australians or a group of thirtysomethings may be more significant than our own family or friends. We are intrigued by the ups and downs of life acted out by fictional figures. But a soap opera about a monarchy afflicted by a host of real-life dilemmas is even more gripping.

Through television, novels, films and videos, people are drawn into a fictional world, and in turn are welcoming fictional people and plots into their lives. The problem is that the line between fiction and fact gets obscured and unfortunately, on many occasions, our hopes, fears and dreams are founded on fiction rather than fact.

The story of the People's Princess is one that has had a considerable effect upon us. Here, more than anywhere else, we see the blurring of the boundaries of reality and fiction. Diana was the most talked of woman on the earth. The chronicles of her life became the news of the world. We demanded not only every detail of her public life, but also, especially, her private life. She became the most loved figure, the most familiar face, the most intriguing character in the royal soap opera. The trouble was that what was really engrossing the world wasn't reality but fiction, wasn't the real person but an image, a fantasy. And the fantasy was not one that she was trying to create. The media have always claimed to reflect what people want. There are times when that is untrue. But I wonder if it wasn't profoundly true about Diana. We all wanted a princess story, a fairytale, a fantasy figure who would help us escape from our ordinary lives.

The trouble is that princesses live only in fairytales. We, however, want our fantasies to emerge from storybooks into the real world. Diana was cast as a fairytale Princess but it seemed with her that a fairytale was actually coming true. And because it was something so many had always wanted we went along with it and became absorbed by it.

It is difficult for us to imagine a time when we were not fascinated with Princess Diana, but much of her early life was spent in relative obscurity. Lady Diana Frances Spencer was born on 1st July 1961 into an aristocratic British family at Park House, the Spencer family home in Norfolk. Her father, Earl Spencer, rented the house from Queen Elizabeth II. He served as equerry to Queen Elizabeth, as he had done to her father, King George VI. Diana's early life was spent at Park House and then the family estate of Althorp.

Diana's formal education commenced at Riddles-worth Hall, an all-girls boarding school in Norfolk. Then she attended West Heath School in Kent, and finally a finishing school in Switzerland, honing her fluency in French and becoming a competent skier. She returned to England as a composed and poised sixteen-year-old. As she had a natural affinity with children she subsequently became a nursery school assistant in London.

A media sensation was born on 24th February 1981. Prince Charles and Lady Diana announced their engagement. I, along with millions of others, avidly followed the courtship of Charles and Diana. At the official engagement, loud cheers rang out in Parliament, and Prince Charles' old minesweeper, *HMS Bronington*, fired off a twenty-one-gun salute. Outside the gates of Buckingham Palace that day, one lady interviewed remarked, 'It's the kind of news that makes you happy to be British again.' On 29th July, the two married in a magnificent ceremony in St Paul's Cathedral. Televised live to millions around the world, it was a 'fairytale wedding'.

This appeared to confirm that fairytales did indeed come true. Cinderella did get to the ball. How we loved Diana when she walked up the aisle towards her Prince, dressed in shining ivory silk, her face half visible behind the drift of her veil, the train of her dress flooding back. As the organ music swelled, our hearts were overflowing. Her Prince was a man of restraint and rectitude. When, on the balcony of Buckingham Palace, he kissed her, she became the sleeping beauty awoken to a new world by her lover. The world swooned and we all wondered: Will they live happily ever after?

Onlookers perceived a fairytale unfolding; the reality, however, was starkly different. For Diana, even then, the situation was heart-breakingly complicated: she wanted to be domestic. For most women the dream of Cinderella becomes the harsh reality Snow White encountered. Most brides discover that if they want a roof over their heads they can stay and be provided for so long as they are prepared to 'make the beds, cook, wash, sew, spin and keep everything clean and tidy' as Snow White did for the dwarfs. But apparently Diana liked washing clothes and preparing meals. She so wanted to nurture those she loved; she so wanted to belong to a family with the normal, ordinary, everyday demands.

Acceptance

We all want to be accepted. The trouble is we want to be accepted not for what we do, or look like, or even for what we can bring or provide, but for who we are. Diana's longing for acceptance was hamstrung by the rigours and disciplines imposed on her as a Princess. She had accepted the title of Princess; she must now comply with the formal duties which were required of her.

Diana's job was to look beautiful, wave, and give birth. The storybook castle turned out to be a cage; she became, in effect, the Prisoner of Wales. The Di, as it were, was cast. It is uncertain how much say Diana was expected to have in the conduct of either her public or her private life. She, however, had her own ideas.

So two people, despite their privilege and enormous wealth, were set on a collision course. Diana did not intend to be a typical fairytale Princess. She was not one to just sit on the back of a horse and let the gallant Prince take her wherever he wanted. Instead of being totally submissive, she began to discover her own identity and to make her own mark.

But above all she tried to make space to be the person she had so wanted when she was a child – a mother. Princess Diana related many of her problems to the trauma of her own parents' break-up when she was six. So traumatic was that event that she remembered for ever the sound of her father loading suitcases into the car, her mother's footsteps crunching across the gravel, the door of the car slamming shut, the engine revving and then fading into the distance as her mother drove out of the gate, out of her life. That profound loss created in Diana a huge emotional deficit, which she was constantly looking to fill.

On 21st June 1982, Prince Charles and Princess Diana's son William was born – a future heir to the throne of England – and on 15th September 1984, their second son Harry was born. This was what Diana most wanted; here were the gifts that were most special to her – not tiaras or crowns, not dresses or even sympathy, but her sons. Yet now we know that, in contrast to fairytales, even though a happy family was what she desired more than anything, this was what eluded her.

Who fractured the fairytale?

Princess Diana caught our attention first in her supporting role in the royal pageant, then as the lead player. Finally she pulled back the curtain to reveal the backstage shenanigans, depriving the show of its magic. In an earlier era, she would have been beheaded, like other inconvenient women with temporal ties with the throne.

After many centuries during which royal foibles had been kept under wraps, the lid was finally off. A royal flush of hearts – Prince Charles and Princess Diana – appealed to the public. The dark side of the fairytale appeared on screen as Prince Charles and Princess Diana gave separate television interviews. A flawed monarchy was revealed.

From all we know of royalty in history, however, the Prince and Princess were not acting in any way that was new. They were not more immoral, or more promiscuous. What, perhaps, has changed is the attention their lives received. For the first time the public were being let in on something that has always been going on – and not just in royal circles but in every section of society, in every age. The storybook Prince and Princess were actually experiencing, in full view of the world, what has touched every family – brokenness. Diana's life, we realised, contained elements from both the fairytale world and the real world we know so well.

We are creatures of the Oprah Winfrey age, in which stars and ordinary people queue up to speak about their sadness, their trauma, to tell their 'I have suffered too' stories. This is what brings credibility. What stronger image for us, then, than a woman who personified our aspirations, yet had gone through the only thing many of us know and can identify with – suffering and pain? In this way, surprisingly, Diana became what the feminist writer Suzanne Moore called the 'heroine of the women's movement'.

Languishing in a loveless marriage, burdened with rigid protocol and constant public scrutiny, Diana fell ill. The Princess suffered from bulimia nervosa.

Modern eating disorders are not so modern, their symptoms having been recorded in the early eighteenth century by Georgio Baglivi, Chair of Medical Theory at the Collegio Della Sapienza in Rome, and by name in 1874 by William W. Gull and Charles E. Laseguè. However, eating disorders such as anorexia and bulimia nervosa have become the women's diseases of the late twentieth century. They are psychological illnesses, symptoms of something deep-seated, for they are caused not just by wanting to be fashionably thin but by a kind of self-loathing and terror of the flesh and sexuality. In 1988, Diana began a course of treatment with a psychiatrist at Guy's Hospital in London. It must have been heartening for her to know that thousands of women went for help as a result of the publicity following the admission of her illness.

In his biography, Andrew Morton describes Diana issuing cries for help with slashes to her chest and thighs. Often it is difficult to determine whether an attempted suicide implies a deliberate intention to die which happens to be unsuccessful, or a deliberate intention not to die but to inflict harm upon oneself. In research surveys, when people were asked why they had attempted suicide, many responded by saying that they wanted to die and to find help as well – they wanted both. An individual attempting suicide is likely to be ambivalent, expressing a desire to die as well as the cry, 'Please help me, I cannot cope by myself.'

Suicide is an act 'prepared within the silence of the heart' wrote the French philosopher Albert Camus. We will never really know what weighed on Diana's heart.

Having suffered much, Diana was able to

empathise with those who suffered far more. If she was no longer Cinderella she had become for her admirers something equally potent – the female victim of a brutal world she had thought she could redeem through love. We had constructed her in the context of a fairytale, and now could deconstruct her in the context of a modern parable about power and powerlessness. There was almost nothing she could do to dispel the image of Diana the saint.

Not every fairytale ends happily ever after. In the summer of 1992, Prime Minister John Major rose in Parliament and announced the formal separation of the Prince and Princess of Wales. On 28th August 1996, a court granted a decree absolute, officially ending the couple's fifteen-year marriage. The grounds for divorce were the 'irretrievable breakdown of the marriage'. As part of the divorce settlement, Diana was stripped of the title Her Royal Highness. So ended the storybook marriage of the century.

When Diana first came on the scene we wanted to see the dreamlike fantasy of a children's story come true. Though through her suffering, pain, brokenness and fractured life we lost that childhood story, we gained one that, as adults, we can relate to more readily. Even those who have been most devoted to the fairytale of the monarchy sense that in the future princesses will belong only in children's books.

What, then, do we do with our need for a fairy-tale? Who can we look up to and worship as a hero? Who is everything we want and need to be? Is there someone who, like Diana, can stand with us in our suffering, pain and brokenness, yet, unlike her, lead us out from it? Can someone not only share but relieve the pain?

4

The King of Hearts

One of the most uncontroversial conclusions drawn from the events following the death of Princess Diana is that as humans we need someone we can not only look up to (and some might even say adore). Alongside that we need someone, like Diana, who has felt pain and suffering and therefore identifies with us – someone who does not stand apart from the rigours and traumas of everyday life. In the summer of 1997 this thought was expressed by The Verve – the most talked of band of the summer – in lines from their much acclaimed song 'Bitter Sweet Symphony':

> I've never prayed but tonight I'm on my knees,
> I need to hear some sounds, which recognise the pain in me.

Mick Jagger and Keith Richards. Abkco Music Inc.

Our reaction to Diana was so strong partly because we felt in her there was one who recognised the pain inside. As we acknowledged in the previous chapter, the wave of emotion that swept over us was the deepest public expression yet of the yearning we have to find a person who will identify with the pain of the world. But what we need is not just someone to stand with us in this, but someone who will lead us from it, who will save us from it. Reassuring though it is to know we are not alone in our suffering, what we need is a way out. As the great fourth-century theologian Gregory of Nazianzus said, 'We celebrate not our sickness but our cure.'

In Diana people did find one whom they could admire and emulate. She also seemed to know the depth of isolation, brokenness and pain which many experience in life. But she could not take us away from it. Nor could the knowledge of her plight bring relief to our lives.

The King of Hearts made such an impact on history that he split it into two, dividing it into two periods – the first before his coming, and the second after it. His name – Jesus Christ. Jesus is not the Queen of Hearts but the King of Love. Jesus is not the People's Princess but the Prince of Peace.

Some general comparisons can be made between the life of Jesus and that of Diana: he died in his thirties, he was no stranger to suffering and pain, he was seen as a threat by some establishment figures, and his life was always and will always be viewed differently by different people. Jesus is another person about whom nearly everyone has an opinion.

Whatever one's view, Jesus Christ is certainly fascinating and without doubt the most important person the world has ever seen. He transcends the categories into which we put others we admire who are now dead.

Of all the men and women who have come and gone in history, some are vaguely remembered and most entirely forgotten. At the time of our life it is impossible to know if we will be remembered in the future. But Jesus has been remembered; indeed, he has been given the most prominent place in history. This is all the more remarkable because from a human point of view he was a public failure and died a disgraceful death. Hardly anyone stayed with him right to the end, and there were only two friends at his burial. He died in shame and humiliation. So the fact that he was to become the most famous person in the world's history would have been absolutely unbelievable to those who stood and watched him being executed on a Friday in Jerusalem nearly 2,000 years ago.

Jesus, like Diana, was used to rejection and being made to feel an outsider. Some of his contemporaries were scandalised by him. Others wrote him off as foolish. Even some of his relatives thought he was out of his mind. Yet he, like Diana, was also admired, loved and adored by many.

Jesus is the reason why Christianity is alive and thriving in the world today. But there are no photos of him, no videos, no interviews, no recordings of his voice. All we have are four brief accounts of his life, and they give a third of their space to the way that he died. So the fact that this obscure man, who lived in the northern regions of Palestine, is the most pivotal person in history is extraordinary. Think about it: he scarcely ever went beyond the confines of his own land, yet his teachings have influenced the thinking and the lives of millions throughout the history of the world.

Though Jesus never wrote a book, in the last century alone over 100,000 books have been written about him. Has his attraction anything to do with his family connections? Not at all! He was born in an ordinary village, the child of a peasant woman, and grew up on a tiny strip of land on the eastern shore of the Mediterranean, not rich in natural resources and of no particular value except as a land bridge between Mesopotamia and Egypt.

Jesus Christ was quite normal and ordinary – at times weary, and always very human. This is entirely to be expected because the truly human finds its fulfilment in Jesus. A story in the Bible describes how Jesus arrived at a well in Samaria and had to sit down because he was so tired. Sometimes we meet people who constantly rush about without getting tired or losing their energy. Jesus was certainly not like that. It is significant that in fact the very actions for which he was most frequently criticised were the actions which actually showed him to be a normal man. When John the Baptist – the messenger sent to prepare people for Jesus – came preaching, the crowd noticed he did not drink and did not eat what they ate. So they complained that he was too severe. Yet when Jesus was observed eating and drinking, people said, 'Here is a glutton and a drunkard, a friend of tax collectors and "sinners"' (Matthew 11:19). Jesus, the only perfect person in history, attracted the notoriously imperfect. He also often caused a stir by his physical contact with those regarded as untouchables.

But we must not imagine Jesus as someone who was never disturbed and never angry, for this is not the picture presented in the Bible. In the Bible we see a man whose indignation at times blazed forth even against his own followers. When his disciples held back mothers who were bringing their children to him, he reproved them sternly with these words: 'Let the little children come to me, and do not hinder them, for the kingdom of God belongs to such as these' (Mark 10:14). Jesus then hugged the children and blessed them.

His anger was particularly strong against those who attempted to come between God and men, women and children. Making a whip out of some cord, he drove them all out of the Temple, including the cattle and sheep intended for sacrifice. He scattered the money-changers' coins, knocked their tables over and said to those selling doves, 'Get these out of here! How dare you turn my Father's house into a market!' (John 2:16).

Jesus never knew earthly luxury. He was born in a stable and at death had nothing but the clothes on his back – and he was stripped even of these. Between these two points he lived a life which he summed up in this way: 'Foxes have holes and birds of the air have nests, but the Son of Man has nowhere to lay his head' (Matthew 8:20). But the irony is that this man who seemed to have nothing, actually had everything. He was the freest man, the most human human being who has ever lived. He was free to be the person he was made to be, not living in terror of what others would think, not living with the fear of being found out. He was free to enjoy what was best in life. So it would be inaccurate to see in Jesus one who did not understand and experience human joy. He had a great time at a wedding in Cana. In fact, he made more wine – gallons of it – just so that the guests could continue their celebration!

His friends included the propertied Nicodemus and Joseph of Arimathea, the rich bureaucrats Zacchaeus and Matthew, the family who entertained him at Bethany, and the wealthy ladies who provided for him and his disciples. However, he did not seek out these wealthy friends in preference to the poor. His sensitive heart responded to human need wherever he encountered it.

Often we overlook Jesus' emotions. He felt compassion, but he could be angry and indignant. At times he was troubled, greatly distressed, very sorrowful, deeply moved and grieved. He sighed, he wept so much that he sobbed, he groaned. He knew what it was to be in agony, but he also rejoiced and was full of joy. And he loved greatly. Jesus reveals what it means to be really human – made in the image of God, without any deficiency or distortion.

When the Bible tells us that Jesus 'felt compassion' it is translating a Greek word that literally means having a sensation in the guts. But it was used to express an emotional sensation – just as we speak of 'heart-breaking', 'head-spinning' or 'gut-wrenching' feelings today.

Like Princess Diana, Mother Teresa, and many others who have touched our hearts, Jesus felt compassion for people in need. His compassion was stirred both by spiritual and physical needs. Human misery in any form always called forth a sympathetic response in Jesus. The sick and the handicapped he took to heart, and he was always there to take the part of the poor. Jesus touched lepers and mixed with the socially disreputable. One of the most characteristic qualities of Jesus was this ability of his to live for others. In the words of St Paul, in the Bible, 'Even Christ did not please himself' (Romans 15:3). He was truly a man for others. His heart broke when he saw people who were downcast and deeply distressed – like sheep without a shepherd. Jesus truly loved. Love is an unshakeable commitment of the will. Love transcends feelings and keeps on going when feelings falter or vanish.

In Bethany he stood beside a tomb, disturbed and weeping because he had lost his friend Lazarus. When the word 'disturbed' was used for animal sounds, it denoted the loud angry snorting of horses. However, when used for human emotions, it expressed the cries of anguish and rage. Jesus wept. His groans welled up from the depths of his spirit, shaking his body. Jesus raged against death, that terrible enemy that had attacked Lazarus and his family, and attacks every other family. Jesus does not condemn the flood of emotions we experience when confronted with death. He does not force us to stuff them into the recesses of our souls. Jesus understands our fears, provides us with human examples for our instruction, and personally involves himself with us in the emotional outflow of our fears, questions and concerns.

In many ways, it is easier to say what Jesus was not than to put into words the unique Jesus, because Jesus is the man who fits no formula. Our vocabulary does not seem adequate in coming to grips with the tremendous mystery that is Jesus. Jesus eludes our categories. History is strewn with the wreckage of books that attempted to say the last word about Jesus. But their authors made him too small because they attempted to force him to conform to our human standards and human psychology.

The final words of John's Gospel in the Bible record this overstatement: 'Jesus did many other things as well. If every one of them were written down, I suppose that even the whole world would not have room for the books that would be written' (John 21:25). Having spent many hours in libraries browsing through hundreds of books on Jesus, I realise how true John's prophecy is.

On one occasion, by feeding thousands of people with five bread loaves and two fishes, Jesus managed to satisfy their physical hunger. But he was aware that they still had an inner hunger – the hunger he had come to satisfy. So he told them that the bread he would give would nourish them into life everlasting. When he said that the true bread came down from heaven, they demanded, 'Sir, from now on give us this bread.' He answered, 'I am the bread of life' (John 6:34–35).

Jesus not only announced that he had come down from heaven, but that he had come down to give himself to die. For the rest of us, death is what we most seek to avoid; what we are interested in is living. We come, whether we are royalty or not, into this world to live. Jesus came into this world to die. Tragic death is a terrible, disconcertingly premature end. Immediately after Diana's death one of the sentiments repeated most often was how terrible it was that her life had been cut short – her life as a mother, as a carer and champion of the causes of many of the voiceless. And what made the situation even sadder was that apparently she had just found happiness again. All this, of course, is natural. But for Jesus, death was his goal and meant a new beginning. Dying was what he came to do, his whole reason for living. Few of his words are really understood without reference to his death.

Christianity shows us that the love which calls us into being was shown most completely as flesh nailed to wood. The reason Jesus died? Well, it's obvious from the story: Judas betrayed him, Peter denied him. He created so much fear in others that they had to get rid of him, because he was too uncomfortable to have around. The ruler – Pontius Pilate – tried to pass the buck and just do his job. Others simply went along with the crowd.

One aspect of Jesus' death which we find hard is that it shows us the kind of things we humans do to each other. The account includes betrayal, denial, broken promises, false displays of love, fear and rejection, individuals caring more about saving their own skin than another's, and people just going along with what was happening.

To a greater or lesser extent, each of us knows what it is to have been treated like this. Jesus' death shows us how we deal with each other. What's even worse is that it shows us not only what we do to each other, but what we do to God when we get our hands on him.

And so, in Jesus' death, we are confronted with an extraordinary event. Through his Son Jesus, God has entered the very pain of the world. He knows all that we endure and put each other through as humans – betrayal, broken promises, pain, suffering, rejection, isolation, death. He is the crucified God, a fellow sufferer. He is one who knows, who has been there and felt the pain. But there's more.

He came not only to stand with us in our brokenness, but also to lead us through it to new life. He is not only the King of broken hearts, but also the healer, the restorer of shattered hearts and lives.

I am constantly amazed, but not surprised, by the way that God's purpose is often accomplished through events which he can hardly be said to have caused. For example, he did not cause Caiaphas, the high priest, to seek the death of Jesus, nor Judas to betray him, nor Pilate to condemn him. However, he took these evil choices and wove them into his purpose. Jesus went through with it all because there was no other way that the sins of the world could be dealt with. In the words of the hymn:

There was no other good enough
To pay the price of sin;
He only could unlock the gate
Of heaven and let us in.

C.F. Alexander

He came not only to share death with us, but also to lead us to resurrection. From the moment the soldiers rolled the stone across the door of the tomb in which Jesus had been buried, they thought his 'movement' was doomed. But that was not the case. It continued and grew.

The only explanation there can be is that, against any and every likelihood, the crucified Jesus was raised to new life after being dead for three days. He appeared to his followers, he met with them, talked with them, ate with them. Scattered and bewildered followers of Jesus gathered together, and through them the truth about Jesus Christ spread, the message of good news. And that good news is that God in Jesus has not only entered into and shared the pain and brokenness of the world, but has acted to heal and remake us all.

He not only stands with us in pain and suffering, but makes a way through it. Similarly, he is not only our role model, our hero, but someone we can actually become like. Jesus came as a saviour, not merely as a teacher. We have all received advice and encouragement which we really want to put into practice; what's important is that we do so. Jesus not only taught people to be good; he also gave them the power to be good. People need new hearts, not just a Queen of Hearts.

Once Jesus said, 'I am the light of the world' (John 8:12). It was not his teaching that was the light of the world, but rather his person. Just as there is only one sun to light the world physically, so he was saying that he was the only light for the world spiritually. Without him every person would be wrapped in spiritual darkness. Just as dust in a room cannot be seen until the light is let in, so no one can know themselves truly until this light shows them their true condition.

I believe in the resurrection and life everlasting, and I also believe in Jesus' crucifixion and death. I am reminded that while the disciples were locked up in fear and denial, it was some women who took spices to anoint Jesus' body. And because of their willingness to face the death of Jesus, they were the first to see his resurrection. When we accept the reality of Jesus' death for us, we discover the key to eternal life.

Diana was an icon of the cult of celebrity. 'I can't believe the strength of the shock,' said royal authority Brian Hoey. 'Diana will become the Evita of Britain. She will always be a 36-year-old fantasy princess with whom people will identify for ever.' The extreme grief we felt at Diana's death reached danger level when it started to contain elements of 'goddess-worship'. Diana was not a goddess. Elton John sang so movingly about the

'Candle in the Wind', but it is Jesus who is the 'Light of the World' – the source of light which cannot be extinguished.

Jesus secured peace and eternal life. If he is what he claimed to be – the Saviour – then we have a leader worth following in these times. When he stepped out of death he crushed sin, gloom and despair. He is a leader to whom we can make sacrifice without loss, and from whom we gain freedom.

We all need light in our darkness. However much we admired someone who has died, however much they shared and felt our pain with us, however brightly their humanity shone, the light of memory and influence is not enough. Yes, people's influence and inspiration continues to encourage us after their death. We weave the effect of their lives into our own. But we need more than a flickering light of memory; we need the full light of life. Princess Diana cannot be that light; she was not made to be. To try to do that to her would be to turn her into something that was obviously never meant to be. We need much more than a candle in the wind; our need is for a light which brings hope, a light which shines through the darkness of death. Only the Prince of Life can provide this light – one crowned not by the people, but by God himself. What we need is the King of Love – Jesus Christ.

5

Facing the Facts

'It is as natural to die as to be born,' wrote the seventeenth-century philosopher Francis Bacon in one of his essays, and the words reflect an academic's calm appraisal of the fact. Yet no human experience frightens us so much as death. Despite our attempts to ignore it, death is always there, standing in the shadows, asking nothing more of us than to recognise it as part of life and to acknowledge its eventual claim on us. When we are young and vigorous, our own death seems like a myth. As we grow older, we push death away like a person who embarrasses us. In time, death seems to stare out at us from every window. The tragic car accident which killed Princess Diana confronted us with the reality that life is as fragile as a candle flame flickering in the breeze. A small puff can just blow it right out.

Royalty are certainly not exempt from tragedy. Many of us will remember another Princess – Princess Grace of Monaco, a woman who was charismatic, vibrant and sociable. By the age of twenty-six she had become a Hollywood megastar. While filming *Thief on the Riviera* she met Prince Rainier of Monaco, and married him in 1956. She had a charmed life and then a tragic, melodramatic death. Princess Grace suffered a stroke at the wheel of her car, and plunged 120 feet down a cliff while her daughter Stephanie, seventeen, tugged at the handbrake. Princess Grace never regained consciousness, and, after medical treatment, she was removed from a life-support system. On 14th September 1982, Her Serene Highness was gone.

St Augustine said long ago, 'Everything in our life, good or bad, is uncertain except death. Only death is certain.' Of course, this simple truth has been known to humankind from the beginning of time, but its implication doesn't always hit us. It was a very human person who wrote this inscription for his tombstone, 'I expected this, but not yet.'

The famous composer Mozart was finishing a requiem mass when he was stricken with his final illness. He said to his doctor, 'I sensed it all the time. My last work will be played first at my funeral. All this time I have been writing my own requiem.'

The ancient philosopher Plato defined life as 'an apprenticeship for death'. He recommended meditation on death in order to discover the meaning of life. To think of death constantly might be morbid, but to ponder it occasionally makes good spiritual sense. Socrates believed that the 'essence of philosophy is preparation for death'. Wagner even prepared his own grave in his garden, and enjoyed introducing the subject to his dinner guests, often taking them into the garden in the middle of a meal to show them his grave!

Death is an inevitable human experience, but there is a strenuous reluctance to admit death even at funerals.

What we do see is death on our screens. Over recent months moviegoers could watch volcanic ash suffocate a Pacific town, floods submerge a sleepy hamlet, forest fires rase much of Wyoming, and an iceberg sink the *Titanic*. But it is still in a world apart from us.

The *Titanic* has had a particular fascination since it sank in 1912. In just the last two years there have been ten books (including the cookbook *Last Dinner on the Titanic*), a TV film, a Broadway musical, a CD-rom game celebrating the disaster, an exhibition of salvaged items, escorted deep-water tours to the actual wreck, and the recent movie blockbuster *Titanic* (the most expensive film ever made – at a cost of $250 million). In fact, in real terms, the movie cost more than the original *Titanic* did.

Why are we so fascinated by portrayals of disaster? Part of it is the sheer emotion-shaking spectacle. All of life's great themes are compressed into a couple of hours. Disasters can be disconcertingly comforting. They remind us of life's preciousness, that we are still alive.

Commercialisation has the consequence of distancing us from the horror of what happened. In an actual disaster people die. On the night of 14th April 1912, the *Titanic* struck an iceberg. Its hull breached, the liner rapidly began taking on water. The waves closed over the *Titanic* at 2:20 am ship's time, and the 882-foot ship plunged to the bottom, 13,000 feet below. Of the 2,200 people on board, 1,500 perished. The biggest, fastest and grandest ship in the world went to the bottom. It really happened.

Throughout history, there have been periods of interest in the afterlife, especially during times of fear about the stability of this life. In the late Middle Ages, around the fourteenth century, there was a tremendous increase in religious discussion of death and the afterlife. Very much like today, it was an era beset by plague, when millions died in their prime. Now the spread of HIV and AIDS is wiping out whole communities – people are dealing not with one loss but with many losses.

Today, approximately 200,000 people died. Some died by mischance, others as a result of murder. Some from too much alcohol, others from starvation. Some died while still in the womb, others of old age. Some died at peace, others fighting all the way. Death, indeed, is the great leveller.

One doctor complained, 'Our patients expect us to make them immortal.' The Cryonics Society offers people with a great deal of faith and money the opportunity to return from the dead. Its main base is in California, USA, although a UK outlet has been established. People have paid this society large sums of money to be frozen after death and stored at minus 196 degrees in the hope that science will discover a way to defrost them at some point in the future.

This is an extreme case, but these people are not the only ones in denial of death. In our society we often mask anything that has to do with death. This is characteristic of industrial cultures obsessed with material belongings – we feel we have a lot to lose.

Perhaps another reason many cling desperately to this life is because they fear there is nothing more to come. And today's preoccupation with youthfulness demonstrates the same deep-seated anxiety about the future and facing that enemy – death.

Despite the modern advancements in science and medicine, we are helpless before death. Yes, we can postpone it, put it off, hold it at bay. But however many advances we make, even the best medical treatment cannot stave it off for ever.

Hundreds of people visit the crypt of St Leonard's Church in Hythe, Kent each summer to stare at 500 skulls neatly arranged on shelves and 8,000 femur bones stacked carefully beside them. Looking at this display of bones, it is hard to picture the exhibits as people who once lived, loved, laughed and cried like us. These human remains challenge healthy tourists with the unspoken message, 'As we are so you will soon be.'

Death puts one's own life in perspective; we suddenly come to realise how quickly time passes and how much we squander.

The prospect of death raises all the important questions: What, if anything, does my life mean? Is there any purpose to my life? Was Shakespeare's Macbeth right in summing up all human existence as 'a tale told by an idiot, full of sound and fury, signifying nothing'? Is there anything more, or is death the end?

In the past few years more books have been written about this subject than in the full century before. Magazines report the long discussions of learned people on death as well as the drawn-out courtroom debates on a suffering person's right to die. Because of Princess Diana's death, the subject of death has suddenly become for a short time a 'hot item'.

All of us know that we must die, but, deluded,

we generally imagine death as far off. However, the death of the Princess, or the death of someone else we love, forces us to do some straight thinking about death. Diana died at the start of a new chapter in her life, with no idea that it would be her last.

The psalmist in the Bible wrote, 'Remember how fleeting is my life. What man can live and not see death, or save himself from the power of the grave?' (Psalm 89:47–48).

When King Philip II of Spain was dying, he called for his son. Pulling aside his royal robes, he showed the young prince the horrible sores covering his body. 'See,' he said, 'how even kings die, how the grandeurs of this world end.'

Death runs to meet us and we, at every moment, are moving towards it; every breath brings us nearer to the end of life. I have often wondered how those who do not think about the shortness of life, and are consequently unprepared for death, act in the face of it. Life is brief and death reveals the actual value of what we think are the 'good things' of life. Of what use are any of them when all that remains for a person is the darkness of the grave?

Many of us, because it terrifies us, try to avoid the questions posed by death. But surely death is the most illuminating experience we can consider in our efforts to find meaning to life. Neither can we give a meaning to life unless we first find a meaning to death. True values become clear in the light of death. Our standpoint on death is central to our standpoint on life, and both involve belief and call for acts of faith.

On the sundials of some old monasteries are the words *Memento Mori* (remember that you have to die). In other monasteries you will find sundials on which has been written *Memento Viveri* (remember that you have to live). Really there is no difference between the two.

The rule of St Benedict challenges monks to incorporate the awareness of death into every moment of their daily life so as to become more fully alive. In this way, death can contribute to life. However, this is possible only once we see death, not in isolation, but in relation to other parts of life – when we show how it fits into the pattern.

The certainty of our death can add impetus to our living, bringing new power and seriousness to our life. It can wake us up. As Dr Johnson remarked, 'When a person knows they will die in a fortnight, it concentrates the mind wonderfully well.' Most people who have come close to dying are aware of that 'fine line'. They have also learned first-hand that there is nothing like a brush with death to make a person appreciate life.

We are not sufficiently thankful for life, and we do not make enough preparation for death. God has given us life, but death is just a breath away.

Social critic Ivan Illich has said that because our

homes have become inhospitable to death, they are inhospitable to life. What was once done in the home – the preparation of food, the manufacture of clothing, education, giving birth and dealing with death – is now either produced or mediated for us by anonymous professionals.

In simpler cultures, including our own in the not too distant past when community and tradition still existed, people took care of their dead. They had neither the money nor the desire to pay another to do it. Death and the subsequent grieving took place at home, and was therefore a more integrated experience.

We say people die. Princess Diana, Mother Teresa, Sir Georg Solti, Dr Victor Frankl died. The key question is: What is the meaning of their death? What has become of them? Most cultures claim that death is the end of the person. The only survival most societies seem to allow a dead individual is in the evidence of the deeds they accomplished before death or in the memory of those who knew them. See what death does to a person. Before death they might have been loved, admired, even sought after. At death they are a body that must be quickly disposed of.

It may be comforting to hope with Tennessee Williams that 'death is one moment and life is so many of them'. But such a concept is false, even in its physical sense. To many, death comes only at the end of an agonisingly protracted illness, the outcome of which has been clear for years. Slow erosion of the body resulting from dread diseases of the nervous system, such as multiple sclerosis or Parkinson's disease, is no short time passing either for the victims or for those responsible for caring for them.

What is death? *The Concise Oxford Dictionary* defines it as the 'final cessation of vital functions'. Put simply, the fact of death is that an individual's heart stops beating and their brain stops functioning. A doctor, after examination, concludes, 'They are dead.' By that the doctor means the physical signs we associate with human life are no longer present. But does that person cease to exist because their heart stops beating and their brain waves terminate?

Why does death rock the mourners? Why do we long that there should be something more? Whether the deceased is a 36-year-old Princess or an 87-year-old nun, death devastates the mourners. The question 'Why?' naturally arises. Death seems to be a mistake, an error. It is not fair. It is as though something has become fouled up in the evolutionary process. Plants and animals die and that seems natural, but not people. People shouldn't die. Shakespeare's King Lear articulated a universal human reaction to death when, with his dead daughter in his arms, he cried, 'No, no, no life! Why should a dog, a horse have life and thou no breath at all?' (*King Lear*, act 5, scene 3).

The point of death is not a good time to deal with the issue of whether or not there is something after death, and to ask if life does actually cease just because the heart has stopped beating. Business people always take prudent measures to make financial gains in ample time in the event of loss later on. Sick people do not put off taking the medicines needed to restore their health. A person on trial for their life will not delay preparation for their trial until the day of the trial itself. The issues of life and death are important and need looking at now. As St Paul wrote, in the Bible, 'The time is short . . . this world in its present form is passing away' (1 Corinthians 7:29, 31).

6

Dying to Live

It's the ultimate statistic, the only thing that we can guarantee will happen to each one of us. But is death the end? Can we look forward to anything beyond, or is that a mere whistling in the wind, simply wishful thinking? This question is critical because what we believe about life beyond death will affect how we live life before death. A firm belief that death is not the end teaches us not only how to die well, but how to live well. But can we know or is it just a matter of guesswork?

Obviously there are as many opinions on this as there are religions. The question of life beyond death, and the form that that life takes, is the primary question for many religions. The death of Diana brought an extraordinary synthesis of beliefs. What became clear was that we have a strong desire to talk about life beyond death, but a whole host of ideas concerning the form which such a life may take.

There are those who believe that this life is all there is. An ancient saying describes this position well: 'When we die, we die – the wind blows away our footprints and that is the end of us.' We saw, however, in the summer of 1997 that very few people actually wanted to believe that. A number of people interviewed on television and radio referred to Princess Diana as an angel who had now been taken to heaven. Others spoke of her spirit being at rest in a place of peace. By far the commonest reaction was that she and her friend Dodi were now together, sharing the happiness they had known for only a short time on earth. But what is the reality? We all know that something is not necessarily true just because we want it to be true, or even passionately believe it to be true. It is possible to convince ourselves of all sorts of things.

What happens when we die? You don't have to be a philosopher or theologian to have pondered that question. The majority of people have a vague positive image, but not a clear picture of what they think the afterlife will be like. They just don't give it much thought. We are not long-range thinkers. Here we have change every hour of the day. From our earthly perspective it is difficult to consider something as profound as eternity.

I believe God often uses people and events to confront us with the major questions of life. Princess Diana's death made us stop and think – to ask questions about life and death, their meaning and purpose. The many different opinions put forward about Diana's post-death existence show the need we feel at a deep level to talk of life after this life, and also to clarify, if possible, any future form of life.

Mother Teresa's life and work drew us, I think, to the one who can provide the answers and assurance to such questions. She continually talked of the primacy of Jesus Christ, the true motive of love, and the value of every human being, whether born or unborn. Mother Teresa followed Jesus Christ with simplicity and passionate conviction. She said, 'I can't bear the pain when people call me a humanitarian worker. My life is devoted to Jesus Christ, it is for him that I breathe and see. Had I been a humanitarian worker, I'd have left it long ago.'

For Mother Teresa, Jesus held the keys. Because of who he is and what he does, basically he is the only one who can really tell us what happens after death. He is the only one who has experienced death and yet is alive to speak to us about it.

The Bible counsels us to remember our creator in the days of our youth, before the days of trouble come. When a life ends, we marvel at its passing, and should look up to God, who gave it so miraculously and receives it back so mysteriously.

Today, while we still have life, we should honour God, and not shrink from choosing that which has lasting value.

Eternal life, said Jesus, means knowing 'you, the only true God, and Jesus Christ, whom you have sent' (John 17:3). Nothing is more important than our relationship with our creator both for this life and for the next.

The Christian faith is all about the fact that unless we do something, our relationship with God will remain in tatters because we have turned our back on him and gone our own way. But in Jesus he has come to bring us back to himself. Jesus opens up the way to God, which we had blocked off. Now, in facing death, we do not rely on our own merit, but on his.

This means that far from fearing death – on our own none of us deserves to go to heaven because we have all lived as enemies of God – we can actually look death straight in the eye with more than just a bit of hope. In fact, we can have complete certainty. Eternal life is a gift God offers to everyone in Jesus.

The joy we expect to experience in the life beyond the grave is captured in the words of Ben Travers. In his autobiography he said that he did not expect or desire a tombstone, but that, if he did have one, he would like engraved on it these words: 'This is where the real fun begins.' Life extends beyond this life.

Why did Diana live for only thirty-six years?
God knows far better than we will ever know
why she had to leave when she did. We have
been assured that he creates no one in vain. But
God did not create Diana to live for thirty-six years.
God created Diana to live for eternity. He created
each of us for eternity. That is where we will find
our true calling, which always seems just out of
reach here on earth. The Bible book of Ecclesiastes
puts things into focus:

> Meaningless! Meaningless! . . . Utterly meaningless!
> Everything is meaningless. What does man gain
> from all his labour at which he toils under the
> sun? Generations come and generations go . . . .
> There is no remembrance of men of old, and even
> those who are yet to come will not be remembered
> by those who follow. . . . I undertook great projects:
> I built houses for myself and planted vineyards. I
> made gardens and parks and planted all kinds of
> fruit trees in them. I made reservoirs to water groves
> of flourishing trees. . . . I amassed silver and gold
> for myself, and the treasure of kings and provinces.
> . . . This too is meaningless. . . . So my heart began
> to despair over all my toilsome labour under the
> sun. . . . He [God] has also set eternity in the hearts
> of men; yet they cannot fathom what God has done
> from beginning to end. (Ecclesiastes 1:2–4, 11; 2:4–6,
> 8, 15, 20; 3:11)

Our quest for immortality and lasting significance
reflects the fact that God has put eternity into our
human hearts, and therefore nothing of time can

fully satisfy. C.S. Lewis wrote, 'If I find in myself a desire which no experience in the world can satisfy, the most probable explanation is that I was made for another world.'

We have been created by God not to die but to live. Physical death as the end of this life is a reality, but it was not God's original intention. Now, though, we have the option of either distracting ourselves in an attempt to avoid the tragedy of our condition, which is the agenda of our whole culture, or facing up to its reality. However, we should be aware that God is not a passive bystander in this drama of life and death. He has involved himself passionately in Jesus Christ. Jesus told his disciples, 'Do not be afraid of those who kill the body but cannot kill the soul. Rather, be afraid of the one who can destroy both soul and body in hell' (Matthew 10:28). He also asked them, 'What good will it be for a man if he gains the whole world, yet forfeits his soul?' (Matthew 16:26).

Jesus Christ died when he was thirty-three. But he was prepared. He regularly talked about his death. He was saying, 'I am going to die, so you had better get prepared for that. You don't really know what I am talking about, but when I have died, then you will know. When I rise from the dead, I will send you my Spirit, my intimate self to be with you. And that Spirit will reveal to you what I was about.'

Jesus' life became fruitful through his death.

What death did to Jesus is nothing compared to what Jesus did to death. He now holds the keys to life and death, therefore if we have a relationship with him, death becomes not the end of life, but leads on to greater fruitfulness.

There is no denying that death is hard and raises all sorts of questions about the value of life. But we do not need to be afraid of the questions. The reassuring truth is that Jesus has gone ahead of us in this same journey and waits for us at its end. Then there will be no more tears. We shall see him as he really is, and we shall become like him.

Jesus shows us what this life beyond death is like. The life that God offers is physical. How do we know? Because Jesus had a physical body when he was raised to new life – he ate and talked and walked. When we die we do not become one drop in an ocean – we are recognisably ourselves; Jesus was recognised – he was the same person, although transformed.

Heaven is not about losing our personality or our identity. Heaven is about becoming more the person we were made to be. One of the main pictures Jesus uses of heaven is of a banquet. Jesus characterises heaven as a place of celebration, parties, dances and feasts.

Heaven has got nothing to do with harps and clouds but everything to do with joy and true life. Martin Luther wrote, 'If you are not allowed to laugh in heaven, I don't want to go there.' God, who created the world, who paints the sunrise with a flick of his wrist, will keep us occupied for eternity without any problem.

Since we can be sure about this, Christians do not need to fear death. Life with Jesus Christ is an endless hope; without him it is a hopeless end. For the Christian, heaven is not a goal; it is a destination. The apostle Paul had discovered this. He said, 'For to me, to live is Christ and to die is gain' (Philippians 1:21).

But a belief in God's gift of resurrection and eternal life does not do away with the pain of parting and the horror of tragic accidents.

As I approach my fortieth birthday, I am trying not to think any more about questions such as 'What can I still do in the years I have left?' or 'How much can I still accomplish?' For me the question is changing from 'How much can I do before I die?' to 'What way of living in these coming years is going to ensure that my death is fruitful?' and 'How can I live in the light of eternity?'

The obituaries have become one of my favourite sections of the newspaper. I enjoy the little stories that emerge from the obituaries of all sorts of people. This has made me think about my own obituary. How many words is a life worth? Mark Twain was remarkably good-humoured about his own premature obituary, using his most famous witticism: 'The reports of my death are greatly exaggerated.'

The founder of the Nobel prize, Alfred Nobel, had the bizarre experience of reading his own obituary when his brother Ludwig died in 1888. A journalist, who mistakenly identified the deceased as Alfred, published his obituary instead. Alfred Bernard Nobel was able to see written before him a summary of the achievements of his life. Materially, it had been a great success – he was very rich. He was a scientific genius; he invented dynamite together with the even more potent solution blasting gelatine, and in 1880 he patented an almost smokeless gunpowder that European armies rushed to buy. In his obituary he was described as 'the merchant of death'. Alfred Nobel was shocked. Was this all his life had been about? Enabling humankind to destroy itself more efficiently?

This chilling incident caused Nobel to work for world peace. He also rewrote his will. He instructed his executors to convert all his remaining property to cash (it came to $9 million) and to invest it in safe securities, the interest from which would be awarded annually in five prizes to those persons who had contributed most to the benefit of humankind during the preceding year. The five categories were physics, chemistry, medicine, literature, and peace. (A prize for economics was added in 1968.) Alfred Nobel died on 10th December 1896. It took more than three years for the legal dust stirred up by Nobel's testament to settle. By

1900, however, the machinery was finally in place for selection of the first Nobel prize-winners, who were named a year later. Since then over 600 Nobel laureates have been recognised. Would there have been a Nobel prize if Alfred Nobel had not read his own obituary? How will my own be summed up in 500 words? How will yours be summed up? Pleasant or unpleasant?

George Bernard Shaw wrote some of the most well known plays of the modern age. As his life was nearing its end, a reporter challenged him to engage in a round of the 'What if?' game.

'Mr Shaw,' he began, 'you have been around some of the most famous people in the world. You are on first-name terms with royalty, world-renowned authors, artists and dignitaries from every continent. If you had your life to live over again and could be anybody you've ever known, who would you want to be?' Shaw thought for a moment and then replied, 'Sir, I would choose to be the man George Bernard Shaw could have been, but never was.'

Mother Teresa and, to a lesser extent, Princess Diana, connected with the Beatitudes of Jesus, 'Blessed are the poor' and 'Blessed are the gentle' – and somehow caught the blessing. As we reach out to the hurting and helpless – people who are dying – we realise they are telling us about the enormous fragility of human existence and the limitations and shortness of our mortal life. Yet stran-

gely enough, through these limitations and
through this brokenness, we get in touch with the
reality of God that transcends chronology. It makes
me believe even more that there is something
beyond, and that it is very real – that it is more
real than what I see today.

The last President of the USSR to rule for any
considerable length of time was Leonid Brezhnev.
When he died he was honoured with a full state
funeral in Red Square. The whole of Moscow
turned out to see him buried, along with hundreds of diplomats and representatives from other
governments.

As his coffin disappeared into the grave, his
widow stood by it, and, in full view of the world,
crossed herself. At the funeral of a man who had
denied God by everything he stood for, held at the
centre of the communist state which had atheism
written into its constitution, the widow crossed
herself. What she had previously had confidence
in was shown, in the experience of death, to be
useless. What do we have confidence in?

The philosopher Blaise Pascal wrote:

> Those who live as if there was no afterlife will gain
> nothing if they are proved to be right and will lose
> everything if they are proved to be wrong. Those who
> live as if the present influences the next world have
> lost nothing if they are proved to be wrong, and will
> have gained everything if they are proved to be right.

7

Preserve Us from Dying Unprepared

In one of the ancient prayers of the Christian church, people ask for God's protection and deliverance: 'From famine and disaster; from violence, murder and dying unprepared, good Lord, deliver us.' Yet generally death is the one thing we spend our life trying not to prepare for.

The famous Christian saint, Francis of Assisi, was hoeing his garden when someone asked what he would do if he were to learn that he would die before sunset. 'I would finish hoeing my garden,' he replied. Francis was obviously prepared to meet his maker. Winston Churchill remarked, 'I am ready to meet my maker; whether my maker is prepared for the ordeal of meeting me is another matter.'

It is very moving to see someone who is able to

look death in the face with dignity and courage. The writer C. S. Lewis said that one of the greatest gifts Christians could give to society was showing people not so much how to live, but how to die. So how should we prepare?

One of the legacies of the events of 31st August 1997 is that once again in the public arena it has become possible to talk about the religious questions raised regarding death. Paul Johnson, writing in *The Daily Mail*, observed that the ocean of grief from ordinary people 'was startling evidence of the need for something numinous, religious, extraterrestrial and definitive in their lives'.

As was so often the case during Diana's life, she has once more achieved far more than she could ever have realised. The nation has undergone a profound religious experience.

Today, in our society, there are many different so-called spiritualities around. But as far as the Bible is concerned, to use the word 'spiritual' as we do now is to misuse it. The respected New Testament expert Professor Gordon Fee points out that when the Bible uses the word 'spiritual' it never uses it in the sense which has become common today. We have become used to the word 'spiritual' meaning anything religious, non-material, other-worldly. But in fact there is not a single instance of it meaning this in the Bible. The word 'spirit' and 'spiritual' is always used in the context of the Spirit of the living God. So what was being shown in those times? Was it really spiritual? Was it caused by the Spirit of God, or was it some out-of-focus, misguided and misplaced religious emotion? Was it the religious dimension of Diana's life which provoked these waves of expression?

As a member of the aristocracy, Diana was brought up with a nodding regard for the established church. While she was a pupil at West Heath School in Kent she was confirmed as a Christian in the Church of England. She was married in St Paul's Cathedral, and, while a member of the Royal family, regularly attended church on state and family occasions. Her sons, William and Harry, were baptised. In public addresses and in letters of support she would often allude to praying, to trusting and desiring God's blessing on people and projects.

However, as is common, this brand of traditional Anglican Christianity was easily mixed with other religious and spiritual causes. In this she shared with her husband, Prince Charles, who made no secret of his attitude to syncretism – the technical term for what my friend and Cambridge theological college principal Graham Cray calls a 'pick and mix attitude to religion, faith and all things spiritual'. You take what you want, and do whatever works for you.

So it did not seem too much of a surprise when a few weeks before her death, the Princess and Dodi Fayed flew by helicopter to Derbyshire to consult a psychic about their future. The visit was evidence that a wide range of beliefs influenced the officially Anglican Princess. Although Diana dabbled in lots of things which the mainstream Christian church would find unacceptable, she never seemed to see the contradiction. She was in this way, as in many others, thoroughly representative of her generation.

The Anglican chaplain in Paris said prayers over her body soon after her death. The Pitié Salpétrière hospital summoned the Venerable Martin Draper, who is Chaplain of St George's Church and Archdeacon of France, early on Sunday morning. In the presence of the British ambassador, he said the traditional prayers of commendation for the departed from the *Book of Common Prayer*.

Rather than papering over the ambiguities of Diana's faith during her life, maybe we should deal with the questions they raise. And instead of simply proclaiming the events at the time of her funeral as evidence of a much longed for and needed spiritual awakening in the country, perhaps we should accept that a far more sober reading is required.

One of the most saddening things about the day Diana died was what happened when the Royal family went to church. On the one hand, it was a wonderful testimony to the faith of the Queen and the rest of the Royal family that church was too important to miss at such a tragic time. But on the other, when the details of the service they had attended became known, who could have not been confused, for there was no mention of the tragedy at all. While this may have been due to the stiff upper lip approach to difficult situations, it says nothing about God's involvement, care and concern for the things which we are going through. It almost gave the signal: go to church if you want to avoid facing the reality and tragedy of life. Is church, after all is said and done, simply an escape?

But there were other signals too. The BBC showed the evening service from St Paul's Cathedral live on the Sunday. While the service was being held, the plane carrying the body of the Princess landed at the air base RAF Northolt, and instead of cutting the service they juxtaposed the singing of the psalm with pictures of the coffin being brought out of the aircraft.

Britain no longer knows much about Christianity. If the nation were truly Christian, certain misunderstandings would not have arisen. The suggestion that it was inappropriate for Princess Diana's sons, Prince William and Prince Harry, to go to church on the morning of their mother's death clearly indicated that some people do not believe in Jesus Christ. And many of the cries for the Royal family to display their grief more openly came from people who obviously were unaware that, for a Christian, the funeral in church is the place for a public display of grief. A practising Christian responds to sorrow by praying to Jesus Christ, for it is Jesus Christ who hears the cry of the human heart that mourns.

The funeral service of Princess Diana took place in Westminster Abbey. The Abbey is a Christian place of worship, where a Christian belief, faith and hope is offered. The Princess of Wales received a Christian funeral and a Christian burial.

Diana's body lies at rest at Althorp Park, her family's ancestral home. Diana moved to Althorp at the age of fourteen when her father, the eighth Earl Spencer, inherited the 550-acre estate from his father. The remains of twenty generations of Spencers, reaching back to 1522, lie in the family vault in the church of St Mary the Virgin in Great Brington. However, the family, concerned that the village would be overwhelmed by visitors, decided to bury Diana on an island in an ornamental lake in the estate's grounds. There, as her brother said, 'her grave can be properly looked after by the family and visited in privacy by her sons'.

The Right Reverend Ian Cundy, Bishop of Peterborough, consecrated the site for Christian burial. Now people make their pilgrimage to the shrine of 'the lady of the lake', the first of many shrines to Diana. In contrast, former theological principal, Dr John Goldingay, points out that the New Testament faith has no holy places or shrines; the empty tomb of Jesus is not central to the Christian faith, but the risen Lord.

The week Britain prayed

Princess Diana's Sunday morning death commenced a week in which Britain's dormant Christianity re-emerged publicly. Where else were people supposed to turn? Prayer and open religiosity accompanied the greatest outpouring of grief in decades. People surprised themselves by becoming religious and spontaneously praying.

Recent statistics of the Church of England are not as bad as the media make out. In fact, more Anglican churches opened than closed last year. And while only 12 per cent of the country attend church regularly, the latest figures indicate that 76 per cent of the nation pray regularly. But is that good enough? Can we all breathe a sigh of relief, and declare ourselves full of faith in God?

At the funeral service for Diana, millions of people joined in with the prayer Jesus taught his disciples, the Lord's Prayer. What did we pray? And did we mean it? The sixty-five words in the Lord's Prayer concisely sum up God's priorities; the prayer is a cry to go back to basics. Could this prayer prayed by millions bring about a spiritual awakening? William Temple, a former Archbishop of Canterbury, wrote, 'People tell me that answers to prayer are merely coincidences. I can only reply that when I pray coincidences happen, and when I don't pray they don't happen.' Before we consider what we all prayed, let us ask ourselves why we prayed it.

On the face of it, that's an easy one. We prayed the Lord's Prayer because it is one of the few things we all share. Alongside the national anthem, and not knowing which way up the Union Jack should go, being able to repeat the Lord's Prayer is what Britons have in common. But it is familiar only because of Britain's Christian heritage. And it is the best known prayer because of the person who taught it.

In one of the accounts we have of Jesus giving the words of the prayer, it is obvious that the disciples have watched him pray and seen something in him they want for themselves. So they ask him to teach them how to pray, and in response he gives them this set of words. It is natural for us to assume, then, that this was exactly how Jesus himself prayed. These words sum up what he most wanted to pass on from his own prayers to those who followed him. And if this is what he prayed, it must show us the things that were most important, indeed vital, for him.

When we are starting to study music we need someone to teach us how to read music, play and sing; we need to learn from an expert. It is the same with prayer. And by studying the Lord's Prayer, we are learning from the expert, Jesus himself. I would rather have an experienced guide than a detailed map. A good guide may not inform me how I am going to arrive at the desired destination, but he will give me directions when needed. Best of all, a guide is a companion on the journey.

What did we pray?

'Our Father in heaven'

We live in the middle of a religious supermarket. Just as in our local supermarket we find many foods from all over the world, so in our culture today we find faiths and beliefs from different places. Taking elements from these different faiths and then combining them is what we have already called a 'pick and mix' attitude to God.

But we should be under no illusions. The words at the start of this prayer indicate that we are not entering a supermarket of faiths with an empty shopping trolley. We are not entering the vague and mysterious world of the supernatural, where nothing can be known about any god or gods. We are not making some attempt to hook ourselves into the spiritual forces of the universe.

This prayer starts by addressing and invoking God – not any god, or every god, but the true God. It doesn't leave our options open. It is not a prayer that anyone of any faith can pray. It does not allow us to give to God any name we might find helpful.

Every time Jesus prays he uses the word Father –
Abba. A friend of mine still remembers an experience he had over thirty years ago in Jerusalem. As
he was walking along, he heard a boy running up
the street shouting, '*Abba*, *Abba*, can I have an ice
cream?'

Abba is the intimate word used by Jewish children when they are calling out to their fathers.
Jesus revolutionised prayer by teaching his followers to address God in such a way. We do not
address the spiritual forces of the world. We do
not invoke the mystery of life. We use a form of
address taken from the closest of human relationships – that between a parent and a child.

That's hard for us, because our society is littered
with stories told by the casualties of bad fathers.
What if God is like my abusive, manipulative,
unloving dad? But if there's one thing that Jesus
is *not* doing, it's saying, 'You know your dad. Well,
God's like that.' If anything, he's saying, 'You
know your own fathers. Well, God's fatherhood is
nothing like that.'

How do we know? We know only because of
Jesus. We call God 'Father' following Jesus' example. God will be to us the kind of Father he was to
Jesus. Jesus had the most personal and loving relationship with God, his Father, in which both gave
and received. And in this prayer he invites us to
have the same relationship with God – to know
him personally as the most extraordinary perfect

parent. There is, therefore, no need for display, no need to convince him that he must listen to us. We can be part of the family – the family of God. It's the family we had run from, but the one which Jesus has brought us back into.

Jesus encourages us, then, to start our prayers by focusing not on ourselves but on God. And not on any god, but on the one who, because of Jesus, we can call Father. For those who mourn, it is wonderful to be able to turn to a personal God who cares for his children and promises to comfort.

'Hallowed be your name'

After establishing the identity of the one to whom he prayed, Jesus expressed his first concern – that God's name should be hallowed. He wanted it to be reverenced and honoured and used only in a way that would bring God glory. The name of God represents the nature of God. To dishonour the name is to dishonour him.

We are talking about the living, holy, powerful God who should not be, and cannot be, messed with, or used and abused, or taken for granted. Rather, he should be treated with awe and respect.

This high view of God's name is reflected in our court system to this day. When people are put under oath, they place their hand on a Bible. Why? They are swearing to God who is absolute truth, and therefore committing themselves to uphold God's character in what they say.

We should not use the name of God flippantly. My wife's name is Killy – it is precious to me. Killy is the name of someone I love very much. If people used my wife's name casually and insultingly, it would concern me. In just the same way, it should concern us when God's name is used in a callous way. If God's name is hallowed, it will not be misused.

'Your kingdom come'

We have focused on God, we've recognised his unique position as holy. Now, instead of getting round to what we want, we realise the first thing to request is what he wants: the coming of his kingdom. Once again, we are orientated away from ourselves to God and his kingdom.

So, whether we are a prince or a pauper, we cannot before God simply pray for the furtherance of our kingdom. It is God's kingdom which counts, not the fashion houses of Paris or the realm of the powerful and wealthy – in fact, quite the opposite.

Jesus shows us what this kingdom is like. It is the kingdom which values those for whom Mother Teresa and Princess Diana did so much work. It's the kingdom belonging to those who followed the funeral cortège – those who are most in need. It is for them not because it over-romanticises them or makes them out to be the most wonderful people – not because they are good, but because God is good. God is on the side of the poor and broken because no one else is.

To pray 'your kingdom come' is to hold out the conviction that one day the kingdom of God will be fully here. It is a cry for that to come sooner rather than later. And that, as we shall see, means we need to change.

'Your will be done on earth as it is in heaven'

Perhaps it is the awareness that the kingdom of God looks very different from the kingdoms we are part of that makes us give up praying for our will to be done and pray instead that his will be done. Whether this prayer was prayed in Westminster Abbey or the Island of Mull, in the Australian outback or the centre of New York, as we prayed that God's will be done, we were faced with the stark reminder that we are living in a world where God's will is not, in reality, the first priority of our lives.

Our world is a place where some people are hounded to death because of who they are. Our world is full of brokenness and pain, adultery and divorce. To pray that the will of God be done in the middle of this kind of world calls for nothing short of a revolution. What if each person who prayed this prayer on that funeral day had set themselves from then on to actually *doing* the will of God?

Imagine what would happen if these millions of people put God's will above their own. If the international representatives that were there aligned their countries to the will of God. If the rock stars and actors, the designers and charity workers put his will first. And it won't do just to say, 'That's impossible,' because one day we will all stand before God and he will want to know whose will ruled every area of our lives.

The reason for this is simple. We are on this earth for the very purpose of doing God's will. Far from taking our life away from us, doing his will will result in us living as we were meant to. His will is to see healing and forgiveness, to see transformation and hope. His will is to see the hungry fed and the poor made rich. His will is ultimately the only thing worth praying for and working for in our lives. Yet so many of us pray and then go straight back to doing just what we want.

Sadly, we are often like those in the Old Testament about whom God had this to say to the prophet Isaiah, 'These people . . . honour me with their lips, but their hearts are far from me' (Isaiah 29:13).

Every area of life matters to God – whether family, education, media, or industry. So God's kingdom and will extends beyond our personal lives into our homes, our relationships, into the very structures of society.

'Give us today our daily bread'

Now we get round to praying for ourselves. Look how restrained the petition is. It is not the demand, 'Give me everything I want,' or even, 'Give me everything I will ever need.' It is a request to have all I need to be a kingdom-builder and a doer of God's will.

How ironic to pray this prayer in a country where we are surrounded with so much. How ironic to pray this prayer in a country which keeps much of the rest of the world's bread and prevents the needy from having it. How ironic to pray this in the middle of a gathering of the highest society in the land.

Before the funeral, the cameras showed us the stars, the great and the good of British society and the international community, who were arriving to pay their respects to Diana. Here were people who had everything: the best musical talent, the best political conviction, the most incisive brains and the largest fortunes. Yet at this point in the service everyone prays that God will give them just what they need for each day. Do they not have enough?

The first principle this prayer recognises is that everything is a gift from God. So, for example, whether or not Sir Elton John recognises his musical gift as such, he can sing and compose songs only because God has given him the gift. However skilled Prime Minister Tony Blair may be, he is able to do what he does only because of the gifts God has given him. Here we recognise that fact, so we pray: 'Allow us, God, to have what we need.' The prayer uses the plural – give *us*. Our request is not just for ourselves but for others, that their needs too may be met. The church is the body of Christ on earth today, and Jesus Christ wants to work through us to demonstrate his compassion and justice. We must recognise that through all that was best in Diana's life – that which evoked the heart-felt reaction – God was helping to meet the needs of others.

Sadly, though, we are not always very responsive. This sums up our reaction:

> I was hungry and you formed a committee to investigate my hunger. I was homeless and you filed a report on my plight. I was sick and you held a seminar on the situation of the underprivileged. You have investigated all the aspects of my plight, yet I am still hungry, homeless and sick.

Jesus Christ does have enormous compassion for the hungry, the homeless, the sick, and the casualties of injustice and unemployment. And he wants to express this compassion through us. So the second principle this prayer affirms is that the gifts which have been given to us by God are to be used to serve others. God may choose to provide for someone else's daily needs through us.

'Forgive us our sins'

It is now that we acknowledge our own failings. As we look back on what we have already prayed perhaps we become aware of what we have done wrong. In calling God Father – maybe we haven't always acted like his children, sometimes more like his enemies. In hallowing his name – for the times my actions haven't honoured him. In praying 'Your kingdom come' – for the times that I have resisted his kingship in my life. In praying that his will be done – for the times when I have not wanted what he wants. In praying for my daily bread – when I haven't recognised the giver and even eaten the bread of others. So here I accept I need forgiveness.

Jesus wants to forgive us. That means setting us free. Wiping the slate clean. Sin and guilt is like rubbish. We have to take it out repeatedly and regularly. If we don't, the whole house starts smelling. Most of us have two kinds of rubbish bins. We have the small waste bin that we keep under the sink or somewhere in the kitchen, and then outside we have the big dustbin. Can you imagine never taking the rubbish out? We use the little waste bin and it starts overflowing. So instead of taking it out, we bring the big dustbin in and soon that one gets full with rubbish and starts stinking. And we end up bringing in an industrial dustbin, but soon that's overflowing. We think: What am I going to do now?

That illustration may seem ridiculous, but that's exactly what some of us do with the rubbish in our lives. Why don't we just take it out and dump the stuff on a regular basis rather than keeping it inside? If it's absurd to do that with rubbish, it's even more senseless to do it with sin and guilt. Why hang onto it when God is ready to forgive freely, instantly and continually? Why keep bringing in a bigger dustbin? We must not let it pile up or sweep it under the carpet otherwise we will get such a big mound under the carpet that people will trip over it. Let's dump it at the cross of Jesus. Don't let sin and guilt pile up over long periods of time. Let us keep clear accounts with God.

Let us go to Jesus – he forgives freely. What do we mean by that – free forgiveness? That sounds too good to be true. It doesn't sound fair, does it? For me to do all those things and then go free. We deserve to pay for the wrong things we do. But the bill's already paid. For 2,000 years ago, on a hill called Golgotha, Jesus, who was sinless, took all the sin and guilt – past, present and future – and was nailed for it on the cross. Why did he do it? Out of love. Jesus paid the bill. That's why we don't need to pay it. He freely forgives, but the fact that forgiveness is free does not mean it was inexpensive. It cost Jesus his life.

When Jesus was dying on the cross he said, 'It is finished' (John 19:30). The Greek word used was

Tetalestai – a legal term found on a stamp used when somebody had paid off what they owed at a store. The bill was stamped, 'Paid in full.' When Jesus died on the cross he said, '*Tetalestai*: it is finished – paid in full.'

If we are carrying a load of sin, regret and guilt we are doing so unnecessarily because Jesus Christ has already paid to release us from it. God wants us to experience guilt-free lives. Many people avoid church thinking that they will feel guilty there, when church is the place that will help us to get rid of it.

The Bible says, 'For it is by grace you have been saved' (Ephesians 2:8). The word grace means a free gift. We don't deserve to be saved from the consequences of the wrong things we have done. It's not our own doing. We don't beg or bargain with Jesus for forgiveness.

A little boy in Trafalgar Square was standing in front of Nelson's Column and a policeman was standing by his side. He looked up and said, 'I'd like to buy this.'

The policeman asked, 'How much have you got?' '75p,' the boy replied.

'Well, that's not enough,' the policeman told him. The boy responded, 'I thought you'd say that.'

So the policeman explained, 'You need to understand three things: first, you could never afford to buy this monument; second, it's not for sale; third, if you are a British citizen, it already belongs to you. It belongs to the people.'

God's forgiveness is like that – it's priceless. We could never buy forgiveness from God. It's not for sale. But we can put our trust in Jesus Christ and discover what is already ours. Forgiveness is ours to experience.

'As we forgive those who sin against us'

If we don't forgive others we lock ourselves in the prison of our unforgiveness and God cannot bless us. If we put ourselves at God's mercy and expect him to be freely forgiving, we must show free forgiving mercy to others. That means we must forgive those whom we may long to blame for Princess Diana's death, forgive those who hurt her, forgive those who mistreated her. If we do not forgive them then we break the bridge over which we ourselves must cross.

'And lead us not into temptation, but deliver us from evil'

One of the most highly regarded plays this century is T. S. Eliot's *Murder in the Cathedral*. In the play the Archbishop of Canterbury, Thomas Becket, is tempted by four figures who try to get him off course. They tempt him with power and influence, with popularity and affection, with financial gain. But it is the last temptation that is the most subtle, and the greatest treason:

To do the right deed for the wrong reason.

In the Abbey in Westminster – when the whole world was mourning the untimely and tragic death of the Princess, with some still claiming she had been murdered – this last temptation still lurked. It had tempted Diana no doubt, and it would tempt the Royal family, and it will tempt us. Do we do things for the right reason? Do we work selflessly for the good of others, or is there a craving for some personal glory?

This prayer recognises the subtleties of temptation, and asks God to help us.

Life is a battle. The words often used in connection with the Christian life are fight, conquer, strive, battle, overcome, victory. Notice the war terminology. There is evil in the world that battles against us under the direction of the evil one – Satan. Let us refuse to be intimidated and request help from God. God is faithful in this. We know because the one who taught us how to pray this prayer was – we are told – tempted in every way that we are and yet did not sin (see Hebrews 4:15). Not only do we have the comfort that God knows what we are going through, but also the knowledge that this Jesus, risen and victorious over temptation, wants to help us. But how?

In the Bible we read, 'Take the helmet of salvation and the sword of the Spirit, which is the word of God' (Ephesians 6:17). A Roman soldier was covered well. A modern equivalent would be a diver's protective clothing. One does not go to the bottom of the ocean without a diving suit. Similarly, St Paul is saying we do not go out into the world without wearing God's armour. We need to fill our lives with God's word. The antidote to temptation is truth.

The Bible contains 810,697 words – lessons from life which provide wisdom, advice, caution, encouragement and inspiration. The Bible can strengthen us, comfort us and help us to make wise decisions.

'For the kingdom, the power and the glory are yours, now and for ever'

Finally, the prayer leaves us looking upward and also looking forward to a God of undefeatable purpose, unrivalled power and eternal honour. At the end comes this shout of hope because we know we are praying this prayer to the eternal God – our Father – who has everything needed to be able to answer it.

And an 'Amen' for completion

This expresses our certainty about what we have just prayed. It is like a personal signature involving ourselves in what has been said. It could be translated, 'So be it,' or, 'I agree.'

Our Father in heaven
Hallowed be your name (*praise*)
Your kingdom come

Your will be done
On earth as it is in heaven (*purpose*)
Give us today our daily bread (*provision*)
Forgive us our sins (*pardon*)
As we forgive those who sin against us (*people*)
And lead us not into temptation, but deliver us from
evil (*protection*)
For the kingdom, the power and the glory are yours,
now and for ever (*perspective*)
AMEN

Millions of us prayed this prayer at Princess Diana's
funeral. The challenge is to believe it and live it.
Doing this makes us friends of God. If we pray this
prayer, if we live this prayer, if we stake our lives
on this prayer, then whenever we die, however we
die – by old age or by tragedy, disaster or long-term
illness – we will not die unprepared.